Jamie's vulnerability will cause you to exhale and remind you of God's grace to build beauty from ashes. Thank you, Jamie, for reminding us that there is freedom in repentance and how beautiful the local church can be.

Jennie Allen, author of *Nothing to Prove* and founder and visionary of the IF:Gathering

Jamie is one of the kindest and most genuine people I've ever met, and you'll be glad to know she shows up exactly in these pages as she does in real life. If you've ever felt held captive by a part of your story that you've kept hidden, Jamie's story will be an encouragement to you that nothing you've done can keep you from living out your purpose in this life.

Amy Brown, co-host of the *Bobby Bones Show*

I'll be buying copies of Jamie's book for all the young gals I know, all the gals wondering how they step into the life they know God has for them. I couldn't tell where Jamie's story ended and Jesus' story began, and that is a very beautiful thing. This book pulls back the curtain on grace, hope, and purpose in a life-giving and encouraging way and I can't suggest reading it enough.

Jess Connolly, speaker and author of *Dance Stand Run* and *Wild and Free*

Jamie's podcast is fun and approachable in tone, just like a happy hour meet up. Her book, while still maintaining the girlfriend to girlfriend tone we have come to know and love from her, also reveals a more vulnerable side of Jamie. She wades in deep waters with Jesus throughout the pages and I found myself dwelling in the waters with her by the book's end.

Jessica Honegger, founder and CEO of Noonday Collection

If you've listened to Jamie's podcast, you no doubt feel like she's a dear, trusted friend. And in Jamie's new book, she takes that friendship to a whole new level by getting all-the-way real with her readers. Refreshingly honest and relatable, *If You Only Knew* is a fearless, bold, gut-level-honest account of Jamie's journey to freedom in Christ. You'll see yourself in her story, and more than anything else, you'll see the loving hand of a Savior who faithfully pursues, redeems, heals, and restores. What a beautifully written, grace-filled reminder that it is for freedom that we have been set free (Gal. 5:1). Don't miss it!

Sophie Hudson, author of *Giddy Up, Eunice* and
All in All: Loving God Wherever You Are

Real, raw, and redemptive. The words that Jamie Ivey shares in *If You Only Knew* offer healing and freedom to women lost in their lives, ashamed of their past, or doubtful that God could still love them. Jamie offers a breath of fresh air to those with a suffocated soul. Her story offers proof that God, in His loving-kindness, is faithful to pursue His people.

Chrystal Evans Hurst, author of *She's Still There*

Jamie is one of my favorite people. She is vulnerable and honest, so of course her book would be exactly that. In *If You Only Knew,* Jamie tells the story of her past and present, but more than that, she tells the story of how God has redeemed the entirety of her story. This book meets people in the trenches of their lives—in heartache, in disappointment, in failure, and reminds them that God gives freedom, peace, and joy when we give those things to Him.

Catherine Lowe, mother, reality-TV
personality, and entrepreneur

Inside these pages, Jamie Ivey invites you into her story about how God's grace led her to experience true freedom, both from her past and for the present. Maybe you, like me, could use a reminder that the gospel not only breaks the bonds of sin, but also removes all our guilt and shame. *If You Only Knew* is the reminder, that the freedom we long for is found only in Jesus, and Jesus is better. This book is the rarest of combinations: both serious and fun. You will be taught and challenged, and yet you will enjoy it all the way.

Russell Moore, president, Ethics and Religious
Liberty Commission of the Southern Baptist Convention

Vulnerability not only makes you brave, but it takes great courage to be vulnerable. Vulnerability unleashes your God-given potential. Jamie's book is refreshingly authentic and vulnerable. She talks about the hard things that get buried in our attempt to make great impressions. We need to hear stories of struggle and how God can redeem and redefine our brokenness. Jamie's honesty will combat the shame that many feel about their past, even our present. I love how Jamie shares her ongoing struggles, but also shows how Scripture guided her to see Jesus in every circumstance. What if we were honest? What if we had the permission to be real? What if we discovered Jesus was better and greater than any of our circumstances? There's something empowering about saying, "Me too." We are not alone in our struggles. This book will be a catalyst in helping others become free to walk and run in the freedom that only Christ gives us all.

Tasha Morrison, founder and president of Be the Bridge

If you've ever wondered if there is room at the table for someone with a story like yours, you'll appreciate the resounding yes Jamie offers as she pulls up a chair alongside you in *If You Only Knew*.

Raechel Myers, founder and CEO of She Reads Truth

Some say that a message is only as believable as its messenger. If that is true, then this book delivers. With endearing and sometimes surprising honesty, Jamie uses her own life story to do what all good story does—tell the story of the God who became a prisoner and slave so we could be made free. I urge you to read these pages slowly and with care. As you do, you may discover, just as Jamie has, that the time to be free isn't later, but now.

Scott Sauls, pastor of Christ Presbyterian Church in Nashville, Tennessee, and author of *Befriend* and *From Weakness to Strength*

This book is a must-read for all! Life is hard; the struggle is real. And most of us have a hard time being vulnerable and honest about our struggles. I am so thankful Jamie has had the courage to address and challenge us with this topic in a deep way! I look forward to the freedom and fruit this book will bring to those who read it!

Cheryl Scruggs, biblical counselor, podcaster, speaker, and author of *I Do Again*

This book brought me so much encouragement to be steadfast in vulnerability (even when I want to hide) and to remember that the Lord redeems all sin and failure and disappointment. Through sharing her own life experiences, Jamie Ivey delivers such a beautiful perspective about the exhaustion of living a life of perceived perfection and contrasts it with the freedom of being known.

Lauren Scruggs, blogger, author, and entrepreneur

Jamie Ivey knows the grace of God deep down in her bones. She tells her story with humor and candor, and with a heaping measure of bravery. I'm beyond thankful for her voice in the church today. I pray that the example of her transparency will spread far, and that the testimony of the gospel found in the pages of this book will saturate the dry soil of many lives.

Jen Wilkin, minister at
The Village Church Institute and author

With honesty, humor, and vulnerability, Jamie Ivey has given women permission to stand tall and be who they were created to be in Christ, no longer weighed down by the lies of the enemy or feeling any shame from the past. *If You Only Knew* is a breath of fresh air full of life-giving truth. I adore Jamie and her heart to see women live free of the weight that holds so many down. This book will help you live free and confident because of the total redeeming work of Jesus!

Alli Worthington, author of *Fierce Faith: A Woman's Guide to Fighting Fear, Wrestling Worry, and Overcoming Anxiety*

If You Only Knew

If You Only Knew

MY UNLIKELY, UNAVOIDABLE STORY OF BECOMING FREE

Jamie Ivey

PUBLISHING GROUP

NASHVILLE, TENNESSEE

Published by B&H Publishing Group
Nashville, Tennessee

Published in association with literary agent Jenni Burke of
D.C. Jacobson & Associates, www.dcjacobson.com.

Dewey Decimal Classification: 234.3
Subject Heading: CHRISTIAN LIFE \ GRACE (THEOLOGY) \
SECRECY

Cover design and illustration by Matt Lehman.

1 2 3 4 5 6 7 • 22 21 20 19 18

To Aaron

You are truly God's kindest gift to me.

Thank you for constantly loving me and pursuing me.

No one else I would rather do life with than you.

Acknowledgments

Two of my favorite sayings capture the way my community has poured into my life over these past two years in the creation of this book—*Together is better* and *Teamwork makes the dream work*. Both of those sayings sum up all of the thank-you's that I'm about to share.

Jenni Burke, you took a chance on me, and for that I'm grateful. I'll never forget sitting in the room with you putting all of my thoughts together and outlining this book on a white board. You have cheered me on with great joy throughout this whole journey! Let's outline the next book in Italy!

Thank you to all of my new friends at B&H and LifeWay. You took this podcaster and helped her write a book! Jennifer, Heather, Mary, Rachel, and Devin, thank you for your patience with me asking eight million questions about every step of this process every single day. Lawrence, thank you for your guidance, your help, and your encouragement! You have all stewarded this story so well, and partnering with you to share the hope of Jesus Christ has been a joy!

Thank you to my church. I hate to tell all of you readers this, but I have the best church in the world. The Austin Stone Community Church has provided numerous opportunities for me to grow in my love for the Word, and to grow in teaching the Word. This journey of freedom that I write about began when I entered that high school gym in 2008 and allowed God to restore my weary and guarded heart.

Not only do I have the best church in the world, I have the best friends in the world. Amy Gayhart, as my longest friend, you have seen this whole story unfold, and loved me every step of the way. Amanda Brown, you make my work life fall into place and I'm so grateful. Your friendship toward me in my career is one of my most precious gifts in this lifetime. I will always say that you are the friend I never knew I needed! Tiffany, Laura, Maris, Kim, Annie, Noelle, Leslie, Suzanne, and Taylor, you all inspire me in your endless support of me. Lindsey and Ginger, thank you for steering these words in the right direction. Angela Suh, you read this whole book and helped me make sure Jesus was always the center of this story—thank you for that, my friend.

Sophie Hudson, your encouragement to me in Kenya has never left me. Nancy Mattingly, I'm convinced no one has ever prayed for me the way you have. You are just simply the best. Shelley Giglio, what an honor to have you write the foreword for this book. It was so fitting since God captured my heart all those years ago at the Passion Conference.

Thank you, podcast listeners, for showing up every single week and inviting your friends to join us! Thank you to every single lady who has joined me on the show. The conversations I have had over the past years have changed me for the better.

To my immediate family: You lived this story, and you never for one moment thought less of me or were embarrassed by me. Thank you for your faithfulness toward Jesus and toward me as your daughter and sister.

My sweet children, Cayden, Amos, Deacon, and Story: People have asked me if I'm worried about what you will think when you read this story. I'm not worried one single bit, because I'm confident that you, too, will see a God who will go to great lengths for His children. The story of God's redemption on my life is nothing to be embarrassed about. I pray that God will capture your attention and hearts young and you will never let go. He's worth it. I promise!

Aaron, you have cheered me on since the day we met. There's not one person who loves me more, believes in me more, or desires bigger things for my life more than you do. You knew this book would happen before I ever believed that it would. Thanks for being my biggest fan!

I'm beyond thankful to the God of the universe who spoke all of this into existence. He has pursued me and loved me in ways I will never comprehend. He put a song in my heart, and I won't stop singing it. Jesus truly is better.

Contents

Foreword

F reedom.

What a *powerful* word.

I was thinking today about a white flag. Every picture and analogy of a white flag has the appearance and smell of defeat; one where your heart is broken that the sacrifice you *know* they paid, and the pursuit you feel like they *must* have been called to and believed in, all evaporates in the raising of the white flag. *We quit. We give up. You win.*

Or do we?

One of the values I love most in the pursuit of Jesus is that a white flag doesn't signify defeat—just surrender.

What I love about the kingdom of God is that it is truly upside down. All the normal is abnormal. All the natural is supernatural. The ordinary is extraordinary.

More is less and less is more. Eternal is significant; here and now is fleeting.

Freedom is a powerful word. It turns out that in our raising the white flag over our life, what we actually experience instead of defeat is *victory*. This is the kingdom of God. This is holy mystery. This is following Jesus. In surrender, we take part in His eternal, lasting victory.

In this book, Jamie tells a "normal" life story of struggle: the belief in lies spoken over her and through her about her own life, which resulted in an existence far less than what she deserved or was promised. Where Jamie's story becomes supernatural is when she places her life in God's hands; when she awakens to the fact that her life is actually not her own. That's when multiplication/transcendence occurs. That's when the kingdom theory of upside-down takes over. Her life becomes extraordinary and more profound and further-reaching than she could have ever expected, all because she raised her own white flag. You and I have the same opportunity in our lives.

Jamie's story moves from a story, a telling . . . to testifying. I hear it said a lot that everyone has a story. I often hear people repeat that every wound and scar in your life becomes a part of your story, and that as humans, we spend too much time covering our scars instead of using them as an opportunity to tell our story. I love all of this, and I agree. Nothing in our life is wasted.

Nothing. However, these stories can often lack authentic power to me. Somehow in the telling, we miss the testifying. We can focus on the scars, instead of on the Savior whose scars healed and freed us.

See, it's not enough that we've made it through our trials. It's not enough that we just lived to tell a story, although for many of us that is miraculous. It's only enough when we tell of the power and redemption of God through our story. Our lives become radiant when we can't help but declare what the Lord has done. Jamie isn't just normal; she's abnormal, because God is in her story. And her ability to preach freedom through her story is compelling!

See, you and I and Jamie all have something deeply in common. We all long to be free.

For me, it's only in recent days that some of that freedom has truly come. As I continue to pursue Jesus, He continues to reveal Himself more and more to me. The more I see of Him, the more I can see me clearly. I am not a mix of seeming mistakes; I am actually designed this way. I am not here to play a role; I'm here as a loved child. I am not just a pastor's wife; I'm actually chosen as Jesus' bride too. I actually encourage and dare you to lean into Jesus and the truth of His Word.

When you read Jamie's testimony of how this occurred to her, I promise you will begin to believe it can be a possibility for you too. You, too, can discover the truth, and that truth can set you *free*. Maybe it's time for you to truly surrender, and Jamie will help you lift your own weighty white flag.

I can't wait to see what you experience in the pages ahead.

I love Jamie, and you will too. Freedom is contagious, and you're about to catch the best infection.

Shelley Giglio

From Failure To Freedom

I've wanted to write this book for more than ten years now.

But I wasn't free to do it.

Too busy? Yes. And no. But I'm not even talking about that kind of freedom. (Freedom for a mother of four is sort of a relative term anyway, as far as having any time to herself goes. I'll catch up when I'm fifty. Or eighty.)

What I'm saying is that it's taken me a while to experience and taste what I'd call *real* freedom. To own the story of how Jesus chased me down and rescued me. And how even today He continues to pursue me, and to work with me, and never seems to grow tired of me or frustrated with me, or with the lengths I've required Him to go in getting through to me and molding me into someone who, I hope, is starting to look more and more like Him.

Ten years ago, I was still too fragile to talk about it. I was still believing so many lies about myself. I was still wearing so many labels, convinced they were all 100 percent true about me. In some ways, I'm just now starting to trust that what His Word says about me is far more important than what anyone else might say or think about me.

My journey to freedom has been a long one. And a hard one.

And I guess that's why I feel so passionate now about sharing my story with you . . . because what I've found is that if I'd been willing to grab hold of freedom, at any point in my journey, it was right there, all along. The freedom of believing that God is bigger—always bigger—than anything we've ever done and any place we've ever failed, was offered to me at every step. All I needed to do was take it. Believe it. Toss everything else out—all the shame and guilt and fear—and just walk on ahead with Him.

The real freedom.

But I couldn't seem to do it. Couldn't allow myself to trust Him. Couldn't accept that I was actually *that* forgiven. Couldn't believe He really meant it. And so I stayed stuck in that place of unbelief, certain I was a failure. When in reality I was completely loved and understood and constantly offered something better than what I was living. That longing for freedom deep in me has been there all along.

I don't know about you, but I talk to enough women today to know that this is a place where many of us are living. Trapped in our past. Hidden deep inside our secrets. Defeated by our struggles. The sum total of our depressing parts. Pretending, not empowered. Fake, not free.

And if that's you, I'm here to tell you this . . . you don't have to stay there. You don't need ten more years like I did to figure it out, to pay for what you've done, to heal enough so that one day you might finally experience the freedom that you see shine from those you admire so much.

You don't need to wait any longer on your freedom.

A young man we'd recently met was over at our house one night. I was out of town, but my husband, Aaron, who'd been helping this guy get into a program to start earning his GED, had invited him over to study and to help him fill out some of his paperwork.

Let's call him Easton. I always said that if I had another son, I'd want to name him Easton, and since the Ivey shop is closed, we'll use that name here. Easton.

He'd had a rough life up to that point. Both of his parents had died, and he ended up being raised by his older brothers who had no intention of pouring into his life or teaching him what it meant to be a man. As a result, he spent a lot of time alone, forced to figure out his own way.

And we all know what happens when *that* happens. He found other people who would love him and care for him. The only problem was that they were more interested in selling him drugs than anything else. Pretty soon, his life began to look just like that of his older brothers, which was the only life he really knew. Some of us go *looking* for sin; Easton's sin came looking for *him*.

So, by the age of fourteen, he was already doing drugs, selling drugs, and basically sleeping wherever he landed at the end of the day. His world became so small, enslaved to an addictive, destructive lifestyle.

Then a Christian family interrupted his tragic world, and he began to live with them and go to church with them. Slowly but surely, he began to discover another way to live. The adults in his life were modeling unconditional love toward him. For the first time, he was living around a healthy marriage and caring parent figures in the home. He eventually got a job and began to work to save for a car. Life began to change for him. He was beginning to find freedom from the lifestyle he'd been accustomed to living.

But change comes hard.

We can still find ourselves resisting what freedom offers.

Aaron was working with Easton and simultaneously keeping an eye on our children, when at some point in the evening, a storm rolled in. Rain began hammering the windows. Noise, wind, lightning, the whole bit. A big, crazy, Texas thunderstorm.

What you need to know about our neighborhood is that whenever a storm comes in—especially a quick one, like that—all the roads flood. What's more, there's only one way in and one way out, which means if you're Easton hanging around on a night when a heavy rain starts up, you're not going anywhere for a while. In fact, when the rain kept falling with no end in sight, Aaron informed him that he was now part of the family and might as well make it a sleepover.

Having an extra person spend the night at our house is not all that uncommon for us, so Aaron knew exactly what to do. Once they finished up the stuff they were working on, he made Easton a bed in the game room, tucked him in, and left to go get everybody else settled down as well. (Okay, I'm most certain he didn't "tuck in" an eighteen-year-old, but I can't help but think a boy whose parents had died so many years ago might actually appreciate being tucked in at night. So I'm saying Aaron tucked him in, whether he did or not. Which I'm most certain he did not.)

Apparently, the storm stayed pretty crazy through the night; kids ran to our bed, where Aaron was sleeping, asking him if they were all going to die. (We might be a bit dramatic in our family, but whatever.) He returned all the scared Ivey kids back to their beds, but he decided, before going back to bed himself, to go check on his guest.

You won't believe what he found.

Easton was sleeping, but not on the bed. In fact, the bed was still made up, just like Aaron had left it. Instead, Easton was stretched out on the ground—no pillow, no blanket, nothing to help him be comfortable—sleeping like a baby.

When Aaron saw him the next morning, he mentioned to Easton that he'd popped his head in during the night to see if he was okay, and was hoping he slept all right.

Aaron said, "I couldn't help but noticing," then paused. He continued by asking Easton directly, "How come you didn't sleep in the bed?"

Easton laughed, a little embarrassed. "I don't know, man. I've just slept on the floor so many times in my life, sleeping in a bed still feels weird."

The floor was still his normal. The floor was where he felt most comfortable, accustomed, safest. It's what he knew, and it's what he kept going back to.

Just like us.

We don't always seem to know what's good for us.

Maybe we somehow feel safer doing life the way we've always done it, even if it's done nothing but hurt us. Maybe we're almost scared of trying anything different.

Easton understood this. I understand this, and quite possibly you understand this as well.

You'll hear me talk several times in this book about the ladies I've gotten to know at the women's jail in our county. Meeting with them each week and serving them has been one of the most rewarding things I've ever done. We're mostly there to help them with job training, interview skills, addiction rehab encouragement, and other things they'll need on the outside. But if I'm honest, I'd say we're *mostly* there to tell them about Jesus and the freedom He offers them.

But I've noticed how talking about freedom in Christ with women who are literally behind bars throws a whole new light on the subject. Most of these women will eventually return to the free world. They'll one day be able to walk out of the jail with all its restrictions and structure and schedule. But to hear them talk about what they expect when they get to taste that freedom . . . they're a little afraid of it.

Oh, don't get me wrong—they are so ready to go back home to their families and their lives. Even little things you and I take for granted are the things in their daydreams. (I once showed up with a cup of ice water from Sonic. The ice nearly put a girl over the edge. She just wanted ice from Sonic again!) But if you listen closely enough, you'll detect a small, underlying fear. Being slaves to their drugs, their abusers, their addictions has been nothing but costly to them. But to think of trying to forge another way of life—even a better one, even a life of complete liberation from what's bound them and harmed them and cost them everything—is a bit frightening. Because it's so unfamiliar.

They know how to live their *old* way.

But this new way—freedom—they strangely wonder if they're up for it.

Although it's really not that strange at all. It's exactly what you and I have spent way too much of our lives doing. Living in the old way because it's comfortable, scared of the freedom that Christ has to offer us.

Freedom is waiting for my friends who are currently in jail, just like it's waiting for us who currently do not believe it could be for us.

Even without the black-and-white jumpsuit, we all struggle to be free.

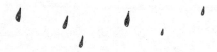

Yet it all goes back to our stories . . . stories that, at first glance, don't feel like they've got any potential freedom at all written inside them. Stories of stupid mistakes. Stories of heartbreaking loss. Stories of glaring failures. Stories of embarrassing, confusing misdirection. Stories we don't always like to tell. Stories we swear we'll *never* tell.

But the thing that's so unclear about them is that our stories themselves are not what's actually keeping us from being as free as we wish. When seen through the eyes of the gospel, our stories are not *obstacles* to our freedom; they are actually the *key* to unlocking it.

And that's what I hope to show you in this book. That's what I hope you'll begin to experience right along with me . . . not ten *years* from now, but *right* now.

I believe stories change the world. It's why I want to share my story with you so badly, even though for much of my life I wanted *no one* to know my story. But I've discovered something: it's by owning and revealing this story that God shines light through me on His Son, Jesus. It's by owning and revealing *your* story that God can shine light on Jesus through you as well. It's by owning and revealing *our* stories—no longer succumbing to shame because of them, but surrendering to God's promises of what He can do with them—that we begin to experience freedom in every beautiful sense of the word.

I know it sounds crazy—crazy scary—but it's true.

I've seen it happen. With a story. With *my* story.

The Bible is in many ways a whole book of stories. God could've chosen to make it nothing but rules, nothing but lecture, nothing but "sit down and take notes," nothing but "drill these concepts into your head." And yet He chose to largely communicate His truth and nature and love and power through the lens of real-life story.

If you grew up in church, you could probably tell me your top ten Bible stories without even hesitating. You wouldn't even wonder if you could come up with ten, but would wonder how to pick the top ten out of the enormous number of stories you've heard and read in your lifetime. You might remember flannel boards and Vacation Bible School, maybe even Backyard Bible Club, where you saw some of these stories come to life for the first time. But if you have no idea what any of these things are, trust me when I tell you—the Bible is full of stories of people just like you and me.

Here are my personal top ten Bible stories:

1. Jesus and the woman caught in adultery (Because, oh my gracious, do I feel like her a lot!)

2. Esther becoming queen (What little girl doesn't love this story?)

3. Mary talking to Elizabeth after she found out she was pregnant with Jesus (Can you even imagine? Virgin? Pregnant? The SON OF GOD in your belly? No space in my brain for this.)

4. Isaac blessing Jacob instead of Esau (Oh, that sneaky Jacob!)

5. Jesus raising Lazarus from the dead (What an amazing thing to do for your friend!)

6. Martha and Mary cleaning and serving (And how we're constantly asked today if we're a Mary or a Martha.)

7. Sarah laughing at the promise of a child (Nobody should ever *laugh* at God!)

8. Daniel in the lions' den (We've seen the lions at the zoo, and no one wants to fall in there!)

9. David beating Goliath (Because doesn't the whole world feel like Goliath sometimes?)

10. Ruth and Naomi sticking together ("Where you go, I will go" . . . Oh, the love in this story. BFFs for life!)

The Bible is jam-packed with great stories—stories of real people who really walked on this same real earth we walk on. They had good days and bad days. They loved people and disappointed people. The women had emotions, and hormones, and periods that probably came on with a vengeance and made them crazy for (at least) three days every month. They most definitely had kids who wouldn't sleep through the night when all their other friends' kids would. The men had egos, and pride, and wanted to punch something when they were mad. (Who am I kidding, the women probably did too—right?!) The stories in the Bible showcase great decisions being made, like when Mary humbly trusted God with an unbelievable secret. And then they show us a lot of poor decisions being made, like . . . good gracious, Peter, did you really need to cut the man's ear off?

But if I was forced to pick another story as one of my alternate favorites, it might be the one at the end of the book of Joshua, where this heroic leader of Israel reminded the people what God had done for them.

Following the death of Moses, God had chosen Joshua to guide the people's conquest of the Promised Land. And not long before his death, Joshua brought all the tribes together with all their leaders and spoke the words of God to them, laying out the whole time line of their history in brief detail. He started with Abraham, Isaac, and Jacob, followed by their descent into slavery in Egypt. After this came Moses, of course, who led the people out of bondage and across the Red Sea into safety, followed by forty years in the wilderness before finally experiencing their promised victories in Canaan.

But let's be honest. If you know your Old Testament history, you know that not all of their days had been good days. A lot of Israel's history had been littered with fear and failure, with pettiness and forgetfulness, with pain and loss. The Bible, as part of the proof of its authenticity, doesn't bang the drum for how unbelievably perfect the nation of Israel was, these people God had chosen to be known by His name. Truth is, they fell down an awful lot. And the Bible is hardly shy about telling it. It's not always a pretty picture.

But as Joshua finished his speech, he took a large stone and set it up for all the people to see. In view of everything God had done, despite their many flaws in the execution, they were making a fresh commitment to follow Him with all their heart and soul. This stone of remembrance was a reminder that their God had been faithful to them throughout their entire lifetimes, and they had promised here in Joshua's final official act to choose the Lord over all the false gods of their past and all the gods of their surrounding culture.

Because, see, more than anything, these stories from the Bible, just like the stories from our own lives, are not the stories of failure. They are the stories of God's faithfulness. When you look at your own story, maybe all you can see are the goof-ups, the mess-ups, the things you're afraid of ever bringing up, even the parts that happened this week or this morning or five minutes before you started reading this chapter today. But if you'd turn your head to look at your story just a little bit differently, you'd see it's actually the record of a faithful God, willing His unwilling child to return to Him, loving you through all your unloveliness. His pursuit of you is simply unavoidable. And His desire is to set you free by His power to forgive, to put you to great use for Him.

The sooner we start looking at our lives and our stories in this clearer way, through the lens of a God who has been and will be faithful to us, that's how much sooner we'll be on the path to freedom. Wouldn't you just love that?

I think sometimes we go through life so fast that we forget all the ways God has been faithful to us—all of the ways our story has twisted and turned for the good and the bad, and yet He was always there, always with a plan for every roller-coaster ride we felt we were on.

That's what this book is for me: my roller-coaster ride. And I'm asking you to get in the cart with me—seeing *your* story through *my* story. This isn't just a book about Jamie, because, for the love!, I would never expect anyone to buy a book just for *that*. It's a book about God and His passionate, relentless pursuit of His people. I've written it for all of us as a reminder of what great lengths our Father will go to bring His children into His family, and then to keep loving us, even in those times when we hardly act like one of His daughters.

I'm not the first to share my story in a book, and I won't be the last. But my hope and prayer for you is that as you read these words, you'll find yourself in them. I pray you'll look deep into your soul and see the things you're afraid of sharing, and you'll offer them to the world as your testimony of redemption and hope.

Because if you are a follower of Jesus, then God is using your whole life—the good, the bad, and the ugly—to bring Himself glory.

Let's offer our stories to those around us as a beacon of hope, so that even in seeing how severely messed up we've been and can sometimes still be, they'll see the One who willingly sacrificed His own Son for sinners just like you and me. Let's not be afraid of showing how much saving we need. Let's show them, through our need, the greatness of our Savior.

Chapter 1

Permission To Be Real

If the table in our backyard could talk, it would share some of the best stories.

Our friend Steven made this table for us. It fits six on a regular night and, don't worry, we can fit eight around when needed. The wood is worn now. There are places where years of wear and tear have chipped away at its surface. The chairs that go around it are a bunch of ragtag rescues from Goodwill. Nothing fancy, and nothing matching.

We call it our Commonfolk Table.

And for a while it was the only table in our backyard, which meant just about everything we did back there happened around it. Steven always says, "A shared table is a shared life," and, gosh, is he right about that.

We've held so many celebrations around that table. We hosted an engagement party for our friends Brett and Lindsey around that table. When our friend Drew proposed to his girlfriend, he did it in our backyard at that table. When we rejoiced over the coming arrival of baby Norah with her parents, Kyle and Annie, it happened at that table. I don't know how many family dinners and Fourth of July parties have centered around that table, but more than I could even begin to count. We've also broken the bread of Communion many times around that table.

I truly love that table.

But we've also mourned and lamented around that table. Tears have been shed around that table. We've sat around that table while one of our dear friends confessed their sexual sin to us. We've sat around that table with other parents, trying to figure out how to raise our kids well. Aaron and his friends have invested many long discussions around that table, talking into the wee hours of the night about all the world's problems.

There's just something about that table. It has a way of making you feel at home, making you feel welcome, making you feel safe.

But I guess of all the eventful moments we've spent around that table, one of them stands out in my memory—a night when Aaron and I were talking there with my dad. I'm certain the kids were already sound asleep in their beds, and my mom was either doing our laundry or doing the dishes inside the house. (Thanks, Mom!)

And on this particular evening, the longer we sat there, our discussion started moving toward things that mattered. Not just the latest coaching debacle at the University of Texas or one of my dad's recent golfing adventures, but real-life talk. The kind of talk that makes you lean in closer to each other, truly listening, not just to the words people are speaking, but to what their heart is actually saying.

We were thinking back. We were reminiscing. About me. What I'd been through. What I'd struggled with. And while some dads might still have a knack for holding grudges over what their kids' troubles have cost them and put them through, my dad that night—for whatever reason—was feeling the weight of his own responsibility. "I think we messed up some in raising you, Jamie. I think I could've done better."

My dad can never talk about anything serious without crying. So as I saw his eyes beginning to fill with tears, mine did too. I grabbed his hand and assured him, "No, Dad, it's not your fault. I made my own choices. I walked my own road. No one pushed me or pulled me in the directions I went. My choices were my choices."

I mean, sure, like all parents, they could've done things differently. Like the time when they discovered a boy in my room in the middle of the night. They probably should have punished me a bit more harshly and taken it more seriously. True, they grounded me. Which meant I had to miss the Sadie Hawkins dance that year.

Which is pure tragedy for a junior in high school. To make it even worse, my friends and I had designed a T-shirt for the dance with all our names on the back. How was I supposed to explain why my name was on the back of a T-shirt for an event I couldn't even go to? Oh, the stresses of eleventh grade!

Or like the night when I arrived home later than my curfew and parked my car just a little too close to the garage door. Well, a *lot* too close actually, because my front bumper put a big dent in it, and I wasn't even aware I'd done it. Maybe if they'd assumed the worst, they might have discovered I'd been drinking that night and had driven myself home. Heaven knows I could've caused more damage than just a dent in a garage door, and pulling me off the road entirely for a while wouldn't have been the worst idea in the world.

I'll come back to this high school stretch of my life later in the book, but know for now that even though I was a "good girl" in the eyes of most people, I was also rebelling against my parents and the rules they'd placed on me—rules, I might add, that were completely normal and necessary for a teenager—a fact I realize even more now that I'm a momma myself!

So the truth is still the truth: My parents weren't responsible for my actions. *I was.*

But Dad was in a reflective mood that night. He was hurting. Searching for answers. Trying to make sense of things, the way middle-aged people often do when they look back on their life.

He was trying to say he was sorry. He was trying to say, "I love you." He was trying to deal with the parts of his life that made him feel regretful, made him feel sad, where he couldn't help but think he'd failed.

In fact, this whole subject got him thinking about his own father and what had happened the day before he died years earlier. He'd never told me this story before because, if he had, I couldn't possibly have forgotten it.

He started sharing how his sister had called to say their seriously ill father was stirring and asking to speak to him. "I'm going to put him on the phone, all right?" This was the man, my grandfather, who was the kind of man who could watch his son go three-for-four in a baseball game (meaning, if you're not too baseball savvy, he had three hits out of his four times at bat) and somehow only find the words to be critical of his one strikeout. This was the man, my grandfather, who withheld approval from his son no matter how actively my dad sought it.

But with his body failing in his final hours on the earth, he whispered the words my dad had longed to hear his entire lifetime—*I love you*. Words that I say to my kids so often, I barely even notice I'm saying them, they're so automatic. Not until that day had he been told what every child should be told *every* day. In my grandfather's own way, he was owning his failure. He was saying I'm sorry. He was trying to be free.

In the days following this conversation around our beloved backyard table, I began to think about the various ways we each try to handle our failures, or even what we *perceive* as failures. My grandfather had failed throughout his life to express affection to his son. My dad, though not actually to blame for the mistakes I made as his daughter, carried around with him a secret sadness of failure that could still haunt him to tears without warning. And even I, right here in the middle of parenting our four young kids— and doing my dang best at it—am making so many mistakes at this gig. As much as I enjoy it, raising humans is the hardest thing I've ever done. Put it together with all the rest of the stuff in my life where I *know* I've messed up, and I don't need any help going to bed at night feeling like a failure.

And if that's you too—if you feel like a failure, whether at parenting or marriage or friendship or just generally at life, either because of stuff you're doing today or stuff that's happened in the past—I want you to hear what I reminded my dad that night. All of us fail. All of us need a Savior. And God is in the business of redeeming our stories so that He will get all glory, not only from our successes, but also from our failures. He wants us to be free.

My story includes a lot of failure. But in reality, it's a story of redemption. It's a story of the Father weaving events together in my life to bring me closer to Him. It's a story of Him redeeming me, not only from big, bad, scary sins, but also from "little" sins I'd

characterized as normal, everyday stuff. (I'm not saying there's anything "normal" about sin; I'm saying we tend to label sins as bigger
and smaller.) It's a story of being rescued from what my disobedience
had done. It's a story of a girl receiving God's grace . . . like your
story is.

I'll never forget the first time I told a friend all the parts of my
story I was so ashamed of—the parts of my story that made me
feel so utterly alone and embarrassed.

At that point, I could count the number of people on one hand
who knew all the stories from my most difficult seasons of life.
Every time I started to get the courage to tell someone the things
I'd been through and the ways God had shown up, I would grow
so timid. I was certain no one could possibly understand what I'd
endured because of my poor choices. I always dreaded they would
think less of me after hearing where I'd been in my past. Would
they only see me for what I'd done, not for what Jesus had done in
me? What if they looked at me the same exact way I once looked
at myself? *What if? What if? What if?* I lived in a constant fear of
"if they only knew." Because if others knew everything about me
. . . I was sure they wouldn't like it.

But maybe my friend Maris would be different.

Maris was actually a new friend, but I had this feeling she would be around for a while. We both lived in the Nashville area, and she was dating Steven (the same Steven who built our Commonfolk Table), who was in Aaron's band at the time. We all knew they would get married someday, and I envisioned us being friends forever, which I'm happy to say we still are.

But before I started to open up with her, I laid the groundwork first. I prepped her for what she was about to hear as if I had spent time in the mafia, sold government secrets, or been a target of FBI surveillance. Cloak-and-dagger stuff. By the time I had set up my story, I think she was actually a bit relieved (or maybe disappointed!) that I hadn't done jail time, lived under a code name, or resurfaced as part of a witness protection program. Although I wouldn't put any of those past me!

Still, I had done some awful things in my life. And as we sat together in the living room of my 1940s-era house, while my baby napped in the other room, I shared it all. Really hard things. I had never laid all my cards on the table in front of someone like that.

You wouldn't believe what happened next.

As soon as the words had finally escaped my mouth, my instant impression was a sudden sense of relief. *I had done it.* I had shared my story, out loud, with a real friend, and . . . you know what? It actually felt good to get it all out.

It helped, of course, that I'd been right about Maris. She gave me permission to be real with her. Although she didn't say those exact words, she was willing to listen to what I said, no matter *what* I was going to say. As I poured out my heart to her, she listened. She didn't try to fix me with canned advice, and she reaffirmed all the things she'd seen God do in my life, even in the short time she'd known me. Her permission that day to be real with her was life-giving to me as a friend. (I'm going to talk a lot more about this subject in chapter 8—about how to be the friend who's listening, not just the one who's telling—but for now, a big shout-out to my friend of many years now who allowed me to be open with her about my struggles, and even in seeing my mess, made me feel loved, honored, and important in her world.)

Another thing I should tell you is I learned something profoundly beautiful that day—something that may surprise you. It's this: our stories are not really as unique as we think. The more I've told of my story through the years, I've discovered my struggles are actually quite common. But because we're all so uncomfortable talking about those struggles—or even hearing about them—we walk around with this idea that no one's ever done what *we've* done, ever felt what *we've* felt, ever thought what *we've* thought, ever said what *we've* said.

This is simply not true.

I'd been scared of my story for years because I assumed no one else had battled what I'd battled. But except for the specific details, many others have fought and lost to the same things—if not *those* things, then *other* things of equal weight in their heart and mind. Think of how much unnecessary anguish and self-torment we've endured, as well as how much freedom we've forgone, from seeing ourselves as the only one. When we're not. We're just not.

But I believed the lies that said I was. I believed the lies that said I was forever defined by my story. I believed the lies that said I couldn't afford to open up. I believed the lies that said all the labels I'd assigned to myself were mine to bear, not to be free of.

And nobody, I thought, could ever take those lies away from me.

Remember the book *The Scarlet Letter* that you were most likely supposed to read in high school? I say "supposed to read" in case you were like me and hardly read any of the books you were "supposed to read." (You'll be proud to know, Mrs. Kelley, I've since read many of the books you said I was "supposed to read" in high school!) The main character in this novel is Hester Prynne, who was caught in adultery and forced to pin the letter "A" to her chest every day. *Adulterer.* The community had branded her this way so that everyone would always know what she had done. She could never escape her past.

I've always felt as though I understood this fictional woman because of seasons in my life when I've imagined a similar letter pinned to my chest. I often felt as though the only thing people would ever see in me—if they only knew—would be the letters *I* knew were invisibly attached there.

Some days I would pin an "F" to my chest. *Fake.* This whole "loving Jesus" thing couldn't possibly be true for a woman like me who'd spent so many years running from Him, disappointing Him, and acting as if He meant nothing to me.

Other days I would pin a "W" on my chest. *Whore.* What kind of girl sleeps around and then thinks she can follow Jesus and be committed to one man for the rest of her life? Surely everyone would think the same thing of me as well.

Many days I would pin a "U" on my chest. *Used.* I assumed this would be my label forever. Because that's what I was. Early in my marriage, I assumed everyone thought this about me and pitied my husband for ending up with a woman who was so tarnished. "He deserved better," I imagined them saying as they watched me walk into the church . . . with a "U" pinned so obviously on my dress.

Not until years later did I begin to realize that the only one obsessively focused on all these letters was me. This subconscious pinning ritual I went through every morning, walking around and thinking everyone else was seeing what I was wearing, was as private as my pain. It was a sick game I was playing. Full of guilt and shame, I was the one who demanded I wear those labels. No one was pinning them on me each day except myself.

I'm guessing this might be the same for you. You get up every day, and you pin a letter on your shirt to define who you think you are, then you walk around with that letter as though wearing it is your job. You think you own that letter, but the truth is, it owns *you*. You make the choice every day to allow it to define you.

"A" for *addict*.

"C" for *cutter*.

"U" for *ugly*.

"D" for *depressed*.

"F" for *failure*.

"L" for *loser*.

"M" for *monster*.

"W" for *worthless*.

"T" for *terrible at everything*.

You pin that letter on your chest as if it's your true identity, when in fact those pins were never meant to be worn for the rest of your life. They are not who you are.

The day I shared my story with Maris, I felt as though I was taking off all my letters and laying them in front of her. I was inviting her into my pinning ritual, even while fearing the whole time that she might only validate my letters as being true. I feared she'd be surprised by all the letters I owned, or embarrassed to have a friend with so many letters to choose from each morning. I feared she'd agree that, yes, I *did* need to keep pinning them on my chest every single day because they indeed represented the words that define me.

That's what we're afraid of, isn't it? We fear that telling someone our story will only make things worse. Even if they're nice to our face, they'll drive home with the shock and surprise still hitting them, still mentally processing it . . . then they'll tell their husbands or other friends . . . then everyone will know *all* our letters, and they'll know they're *all* true. We fear that's what they'll think of us from now on because it's surely what God thinks about us too.

But those are the letters *we've* drawn up. And they don't match up with God's letters. When we spend our days living in fear of what the world would think of us, if they really knew us, we haven't yet believed and trusted the truths He says about us.

If you're a follower of Christ, you've had a conversion experience. Once you were dead in your sin, and then God called you by name, justified you, put His righteousness on you, and made you His child. That's the beauty of the gospel.

There are moments when I can't even wrap my brain around this concept, and yet . . . there it is. Thank goodness we don't need to completely understand it in order to completely receive it and completely live it.

There's a particular conversion story described in the Bible that I simply can't get enough of. Every single story of someone following Jesus is worth rejoicing over, but there's something truly amazing about someone who used to kill Christians and then actually became one himself. Doesn't make a lot of sense, right?! Movie-worthy, for sure.

His name was Saul. (You've probably heard of him.) The first time we see his name in the Bible is when the self-righteous defenders of God were stoning a man named Stephen for daring to say that Jesus was the Son of God who'd come in fulfillment of the Scriptures these people claimed to believe. They "laid down their garments at the feet of a young man named Saul" (Acts 7:58) since they had no doubt "Saul approved of his execution" (Acts 8:1). Saul was known as someone who was "ravaging the church, and entering house after house, he dragged off men and women and committed them to prison" (Acts 8:3).

Listen, Saul wasn't playing around with persecuting Christian believers. He wasn't the kind of guy you'd want to invite over for dinner! And definitely not the kind of person you'd imagine would one day put himself at constant risk by defending the church with his life and boldly declaring his belief in Jesus Christ—the kind of man who would end up writing more books of our New Testament than anyone else. Because let me remind you, HE WAS KILLING CHRISTIANS.

But as God often does, He interrupted Saul's life. He revealed Himself to him while Saul was literally on the way to find "any men and women who belonged to the Way" (a common name for early Christians), so that "he might bring them bound to Jerusalem" (Acts 9:2). One day he was killing Christians, and soon thereafter he was preaching the gospel of Jesus to those around him. The change was so dramatic, he even took a new name. The imprisoning Saul became the apostle Paul.

Let's take a second here and imagine the pinning process that Paul the Christian might have gone through each morning when he was putting on his cloak each day and fastening his sandals on his feet. We'll mention just the big one—"M" for murderer. Because, remember, HE KILLED CHRISTIANS.

Even a tough guy like Paul must have wrestled with these memories from his past. He must have wished a million times he'd never done the kinds of horrible things he'd been guilty of committing. Part of him must have loved nothing better than sweeping it all under the rug and never talking about it, imagining how much more freely he could share and minister God's love if he hadn't maligned and misunderstood it for so much of his life.

And yet his story actually set the table for the message he was declaring. His story gave the living-proof evidence of the salvation he was trying to put into words. I mean, look, his words are still ministering to us thousands of years after he wrote them! If he hadn't been willing to offer up his whole life as a witness to God's grace, someone else would have needed to do it. This was God's plan for what He wanted to do through Paul, and he was not afraid to embrace it.

This is why I love Paul so much. His story is what makes me believe that no one is immune to the love of God through Christ. *No one.* Not you. Not me. Not the woman who drove drunk and killed a family. Not your neighbor who's addicted to pain pills. Not the man down the street who drove his wife away by his constant abuse. Not the member of ISIS who's killing Christians. Not the woman who's undergone numerous abortions. Not the couple who've both cheated on each other and disgraced their marriage. Not the girl who sleeps around with anyone who'll have her. No one is too far gone to be rescued by the love and grace of God.

And while sin does come with consequences—none greater than the consequence of Jesus Christ willingly suffering death in our place on a bloody cross—salvation comes with a new identity.

"Therefore, if anyone is in Christ, he is a new creation. The old has passed away; behold the new has come" (2 Cor. 5:17).

So when God said, "Go, for he is a chosen instrument of mine to carry my name before the Gentiles and kings and the children of Israel" (Acts 9:15), and he has been killing Christians, we can believe that God can say those things about us, no matter what we have done. God can look at you and me—and at all our sins and rebellion He's overcome in us—and see us, too, as instruments in His hand for whatever purpose He's chosen us to be and become.

We are not our letters anymore.

We belong to a new Storyteller.

You may be thinking, *What does that even mean?* I'm so glad you asked! I'll tell you both what it does mean and what it doesn't mean. It doesn't mean our stories go away. In Paul's case, since his cruel reputation was so public, he could hardly avoid the scrutiny of it. Whenever he showed up in a synagogue, the stories of his previous lifestyle had already preceded him. And yet he deliberately chose to own it, not excuse it, throughout the unfolding of Scripture. That's because his story, like our story, is a representation of the gospel. Despite the enormity of Paul's sin, God had reached out and grabbed him and turned his life upside down. God hadn't erased his story; He had actually authored it for a purpose. An unbelievably glorious purpose.

We can learn a thing or two from Paul about being real with people. He knew what was at stake when sharing the struggles of his past with the people he lived and worked around. In his letter to the Galatians, he used his story to remind them just how real and undeniable the gospel of Jesus truly is. By reminding them what he'd done in his "former life," how he'd "persecuted the church of God violently and tried to destroy it" (Gal. 1:13), he was laying all his cards on the table. No guesswork was needed for seeing exactly who Paul had been. But he did it for one overarching reason. When people kept hearing how "he who used to persecute us is now preaching the faith he once tried to destroy," here's what happened: "They glorified God because of me" (Gal. 1:23–24).

They glorified God because of me.

The first time I read this, I choked up. "They glorified God because of me," he said—not just the new Paul, but the old one. ALL OF HIM. God wasn't limited to getting glory from what Paul had finally become; He also received glory from what He'd done with the poor choices Paul had made all along. God had chosen Paul to be a vessel of the gospel before the beginning of time. Nothing that Paul said or did was a surprise to God, yet it was all being used to bring God glory. All of it.

Paul knew something I'm slowly starting to realize as I follow Jesus more and learn to trust His words to be true. He knew and believed that God was bigger than his past. Instead of being held back by his failures, he was pushed forward to continue proclaiming the truth of the gospel, even in how it was fleshed out through his own indefensible mistakes.

Wow, this is such good news for us. You and I can do this too! Because if God could use a man with a past like Paul's, then surely He can use us as well. If God could love a man who killed people who were following Jesus, then surely He can love us as well. If God could allow a murderer to do amazing things for His kingdom, then surely He can use us for His glory as well. We can own our story because it's actually a testimony to the Good News of Jesus, who loves us, pursues us, and saves us in spite of ourselves.

Just as Paul said, "They glorified God because of me," we can say the same thing. We can be people who share our hurts, share our struggles, share our failures, share our stories. And we can trust without a doubt that God will get glory from it . . . from ALL of it.

So just as my friend Maris granted me full permission to be real with her, I'm doing the same for you. I'm giving you permission to let down your guard, to lay down all the pins you've worn on your chest for all these years, and to let God woo you into His love and grace.

If you were sitting around my backyard table with me, and we were chatting, I'd want you to feel as though you were safe, that your story is welcome with me. But since we're meeting instead around the table legs of this book right now, I'm doing the same thing by choosing to go first. I'm going to tell you parts of my story that are sacred and sometimes hard to say out loud because I want you to know you can do that too.

I'm taking off my pins. Every single one of them.

And may God be glorified through what we're doing together.

Chapter 2

Growing Up with God

Just so you'll know where I'm coming from . . .

My parents didn't really start out doing the whole church thing. My mom grew up Baptist and my dad in the Church of Christ, so after they had kids, they settled on joining the local Methodist church. Split the difference.

On a side note: I adore it when parents who don't go to church start attending when they have kids. Some see them as hypocrites and wonder why they didn't feel the need for it in all those years before their kids showed up, but I see them as sweet parents who want something better for their children. They sense this yearning inside of them (hello, God yearning!) to build a foundation of faith that, even if they're not so sure they believe in it for themselves, they do believe in it for their kids. It's so amazing to see God put desires in parents that could only come from Him. On their own, they couldn't even begin to dream up such a desire.

That's what my parents decided to do. And they were doing just fine and dandy at the Methodist church—if by *fine* you mean showing up on a semi-regular basis. But they didn't bring much of it home with them. Nothing in their personal lives revealed a love for Jesus. It was mostly an act. And if asked to do anything more than merely attend church, they were out.

Which, again, was sort of working fine for them until my mom actually *did* start wanting more than she was getting from her current church life.

Thus, she started cheating on the Methodist church by visiting the Baptist church with a friend of hers on Sunday mornings.

Not knocking the Methodists, mind you. It wasn't about a denomination with my mom. It's just that in this case, Jesus began transforming her life through what she was experiencing at a different church. And once that started happening, she knew she'd found her new home.

Only not so much my dad. In fact, with Mom running off to the *Baptist* church, and my brother and I starting to ask why they now went to *different* churches, my dad saw an opportunity for not going to church at all. A win-win for both of them.

Now that I'm an adult, I get what it's like to go to different churches. My husband is the worship leader at our church. We moved to Austin for him to work there. But not a year after we'd moved, our church opened a second campus in our neighborhood—so close that we could walk or ride bikes to it if we wanted. In fact, one time we *did* ride our bikes to church. Let me rephrase that: the kids rode their bikes, and I walked with them. Actually, let me rephrase that again: the three boys rode their bikes, and my daughter, Story, who was around four at the time, *sat* on her bike, which I pushed most of the way, with her on it. Needless to say, when we finally arrived at church, I was glistening so much, it looked as if the angel of the Lord had descended ON MY FACE.

Well, a few years into our separate church experience, the kids and I were attending the church campus in our neighborhood (because, again, it was so close we could walk there *if we wanted*), and Aaron was leading worship at the main church campus downtown. On Sunday mornings, our kids began asking if we were going to "Daddy's church" or "Mommy's church" that day. We tried to explain how it was all one church, simply meeting in two places. But the longer we talked, the less traction of understanding we were getting. Pretty soon we were all making the drive downtown again so we could attend "Daddy's church" as a family.

I guess some version of this conversation is what happened in my childhood home, as well, while Mom was sneaking off to the Baptist church with us kids, and Dad either stayed home or worked. I'm certain my mom asked him every Sunday if he would attend church with us, and surely my dad said he was busy with work (or a tee time) . . . until one day he just decided to appease her and go to church with her.

And guess what? My dad met Jesus for the first time that Sunday. His life was instantly changed. He'd been living basically for no one other than himself for years—drinking heavily, doing whatever he wanted. Then God intervened that morning, bringing him face-to-face with his sin and the Savior of the world. For the first time, he realized he needed Jesus.

That's the day that the hope of Jesus truly entered my home. Today *my* children hear about Jesus in our home, because *I* heard about Jesus in my home, because my *mom and dad* heard about Jesus all those years ago.

Beautiful how that works.

So that's how young Jamie "grew up in the church." You know how you hear people say that? "I grew up in the church." Well, that's what I did too.

I guess, when you think about it, it sounds rather weird. But when you remember more days spent at church than you do at your own house, it's pretty true. From the day my dad started following Jesus, an accurate description of my life was that I "grew up in the church." In fact, even though I have an absolutely terrible memory—just last night at dinner, a friend of mine was recounting the first time we met three years ago, and I swear I have no clear recollection of it—I do believe I could actually draw you a map from memory right now of my childhood church home: First Baptist Church of Brownwood, Texas.

I remember the sanctuary with the organ pipes. I remember the balcony where we would sit as kids because we were too cool to sit with our parents during the service. I remember the big doors that opened into the back of the sanctuary—the kind of doors a little girl dreams of walking through in her white dress on her wedding day with her daddy. (I may or may not have imagined that a few times during church!)

Mind if I take you on a little tour?

First, I could take you to the sound booth. At ten years old, I somehow managed to get onto the church's media team, and they stupidly allowed me to run one of the cameras that recorded the worship services. These weren't like the cameras you see today, the kind you can literally hold in the palm of your hand. These cameras looked more like the first computers that were ever built. They were ginormous, with lots of knobs to turn, and a big viewfinder screen that showed you exactly what you were filming. Just like on the evening news. I wore the big, oversized headphones with the microphone-thing to talk into and, basically, I thought I was IT. (This might be where my childhood dream of becoming a TV personality took shape. Actually, who am I kidding? That's still my grown-up dream as well!)

Next, I could take you to the choir room. My friends and I were all in youth choir, which is really funny to me now. There were no tryouts, and clearly they let anyone in, because my musician husband has told me on numerous occasions that I am indeed tone-deaf. Mr. Stanton, the music pastor, would pick us up from school on Wednesdays in the church van and drive us there in time for choir practice. I made him super mad many times when I wasn't waiting at the assigned pickup spot but had wandered over instead to the ice cream shop to get myself a little afternoon snack. I've always kind of done whatever I wanted to do, whenever I wanted to do it—especially when there's food involved!

Oh, and speaking of food, let me take you now to the fellowship hall for Wednesday-night dinner. Can we just stop right here and have a moment of silence for mommas who don't go to churches where they serve Wednesday night dinners? Listen, y'all, when I was growing up in church, dinner was taken care of. *Every. Single. Wednesday. Night.* Mommas weren't cooking anything on this night. They weren't taking any kids to practice on this night. They were sitting themselves down on this night and eating a supper that SOMEBODY ELSE made for them and their families. Can you even believe that?

But in small towns back then, NOTHING happened on Wednesday nights. It might as well have been the second Sunday in the week: Sunday, Monday, Tuesday, ~~Wednesday~~ Sunday, Thursday, Friday, Saturday.

Parents truly weren't in charge of their kids at all on Wednesday nights, because after dinner we all ran off to either GAs (Girls in Action, a mission-focused program for elementary-age children), RAs (Royal Ambassadors, the boys version of GAs), or if you were really advanced in your faith . . . Bible Drill.

I loved Bible Drill, basically because I love winning at anything. In Bible Drill (let me educate you a little if you didn't grow up in a church like the one I did), all the participants stand in a line, side by side, holding their Bibles at arm's length against one hip, waiting for the leader to call out a particular Bible passage. Once everyone's heard it and the leader says, "Go," the first kid who finds the verse, stabs their finger on it, and steps forward is the winner. What fun!

Oh, man, growing up in church was great. So many moments. So many memories. I remember sitting in Pastor Williford's office, telling him I wanted to follow Jesus and be baptized. I remember the church camp where a girl fell off a wall and broke her arm. I remember Vacation Bible School in the summer. I remember all this church stuff because it was so much of our family's life.

And then, just like that, my life at FBC Brownwood was over.

With only two months left to go in sixth grade, our family moved away from this small town in central Texas, three hundred miles southeast to a suburb of Houston for my dad's new job. You can imagine how hard this was on a sixth-grade girl. All new places. All new people. Nothing the same. Nothing familiar. I was out of my element, needing to learn a new school and neighborhood and what the kids in Houston thought was cool compared to all the old friends I'd known and been around my whole life. It was overwhelming, to say the least.

But of course, one of the first things we did was find a *new* church, and we fairly seamlessly continued on with our lifestyle of regular church activities.

One of the biggest moments from my early years in this new-found church of ours occurred when a group of traveling evangelists came through town and spent a solid week ministering to our congregation. The team was made up of families from Michigan who went all over the country in RVs, doing presentations at local churches. And with programs on tap each night, geared toward all ages, the youth at our church were spending their afternoons and evenings hanging around these kids who'd descended from the north into southern Texas.

Let me see if I can paint the picture for you. This was early '90s, okay? Each service included a lot of singing. All the kids wore matching suits and dresses. I may be wrong, but I believe they capped off each evening with a rousing rendition of "God Bless America." I'm sure it was all meant as a well-meaning outreach, which I'm sure presented the gospel in ways that got through to a number of people, but . . . to each his own.

As for me, all I knew was this: I was going to marry one of the boys from that group.

From the moment I saw Stephen, I was smitten. He was so cute. And he seemed to love God dearly. I was already at an age where I knew I wanted to love God, pursue Him, and spend my whole life with a man who did the same. And when I looked at Stephen, as much as any seventh grader can know these sorts of things, I felt like he was the kind of guy I wanted to marry.

He was "the one." *My Stephen.*

Thirteen, and I'd already found him.

But the cut of his suit wasn't all that attracted me to cute Stephen from Michigan. He, along with some of the other kids in his traveling group, had shared how they made a promise to their parents—and to God—not even to *kiss* another person until they shared their first kiss as husband and wife at the wedding altar. Up until that point, I hadn't yet experienced my first kiss, hadn't felt all the surge of teenage passion generated by that first peck on the lips.

And so, true to my extreme, daring nature and my zeal for setting bold, bodacious goals, I was totally on board with the lofty challenge of saving my first kiss for marriage. I mean, how hard could it be for me and Stephen—in our long-distance relationship—to stay committed to this promise while we waited for our big day to arrive? I was fully committed to kiss kissing good-bye.

Yet life moved on after Stephen left town. We did write letters back and forth for a while, but pretty soon the boys who lived a lot closer started noticing me too. And all my dreams of marrying the guy from Michigan who loved God and was saving his first kiss for marriage vanished in the trail of exhaust from their departing RV.

That's sort of what "growing up in the church" can be like— not that it's a bad thing at all. I'm glad *my* kids are growing up in church. But for me, this infatuation with Stephen sort of signaled the disconnect that was already happening in my heart. Although I'd walked the aisle when I was ten, although I'd declared my desire to give my life to Jesus, although I'd been baptized a few months later and continued to be involved in a lot of church activities, somewhere along the way I lost track of (or possibly never learned) what it really meant to follow God. The disconnect between my heart and my head began to grow immensely. As wide as the Grand Canyon. And all the honors from my Bible Drill days were doing nothing for me now.

You know what I'm talking about? Were you maybe one of those kids too?

Knowing where to find the Sermon on the Mount and truly believing what Jesus meant when He said it are two vastly different things. Spending *time* at church and living like you *are* the church are not the same. By high school I was no longer believing that God had something great planned for me. By high school I'd begun to live two vastly different lives—a dance I would continue dancing for years—the dance of knowing things about God and even sharing those things with others, but not truly believing them for myself, not truly giving myself over to God. I thought this life would work for me. I really did. But over the next few years, I would find that knowing *about* God instead of actually *knowing* God wasn't enough.

It never is.

Recently my high school graduating class celebrated twenty years since graduation. And while I still can't believe it's been that long ago since I was a teenager, the deep regrets that go back all those years are still able to attack my heart, even at such a distance.

I wonder if you can relate.

Regret is such a harsh word for us. It can bring up emotions in us that can seem hard to understand and accept. Pastor John Piper wrote a sermon about godly regret versus worldly regret, and it helps when I think back on my life before Jesus. He said that there is a regret that leads to shame and humiliation and embarrassment, and one that leads to repentance and salvation. I'm certain you can see which one is the godly regret. Second Corinthians 7:10 says, "For godly grief produces a repentance that leads to salvation without regret, whereas worldly grief produces death." Piper said, "Godly grief, or godly regret, is the uncomfortable feeling of guilt when the Word of God shows you that what you've done is sin and thus has brought reproach on God's name."[1]

That's the kind of regret available to us if we trust it to be true—godly regret. This can and should be part of each of our stories of becoming free. So maybe, instead of talking with you about my *regrets* from high school and college days, I should talk about how these regrets and grief led me to repentance and ultimately salvation.

I look back on those years and just want to hang my head in shame for the way I represented Jesus and His Good News. I trampled on it! I proclaimed it with my mouth, judged those around me who didn't believe, and then lived for myself with no regard for the God of the universe. I was like the Pharisees in the Bible—so much knowledge and no life-change. Loving the Lord my God with all my heart, mind, and soul wasn't even on my radar.

I was on the leadership team for our school's Fellowship of Christian Athletes, for example, and the whole time, I was drinking heavily and sleeping with my boyfriend. I mean, how fake is that! It's not like I was the only one, but it still wasn't okay. I was in leadership. I was part of an organization with the purpose of championing the gospel, and yet I hadn't been changed by the gospel myself! My life was no different from anyone who didn't claim to know Jesus at all . . . except that I'd grown up in church, and still went to church every Sunday whether I was hung over or not. That's what I built my safety net with—the misconception that since I'd "prayed the prayer," been baptized, regularly attended church, and was what most people considered a relatively good person, I was safe from hell. I was *fine*. The double life was working out okay for me. I was managing it. And I was safely on God's side in spite of it.

Only I *wasn't* fine. I was enslaved to my sin. This Jesus I spoke about and sang about was, in reality, a stranger to me. I could tell you stuff about Him, but not about how He'd changed my life. Because He hadn't.

Even my life as a churchgoer was a denial of Jesus.

Our family was recently reading one of the passages in the Gospels where Peter denied Jesus three times on the eve of His crucifixion. My kids were shocked that someone could do that to their best friend, much less when that best friend was Jesus. (Isn't that the kind of sensitivity we all wish we felt toward our sin? That it shocks us? That we're horrified by it?) But as we were reading, I couldn't help but think back to how my own life had once been such a denial of Him. On the outside, I acted like I knew Him, and loved Him, but on the inside, I was purely living for my own self—definitely not following Jesus. And in that moment, hearing my kids' disbelief that a follower of Jesus could ever let their friend down in this way, twenty-year-old memories of pretending to love Jesus easily found their way back to my heart again. With a vengeance. Know the feeling?

Maybe that's your story too.

But it brought to mind another story—one that followed a few weeks later in Peter's life, after Jesus had been resurrected from the dead, before ascending into heaven to be with God the Father. Peter and some of the others had been up before dawn, out on their fishing boat, catching nothing but the wind in their sails. Yet at daybreak, Jesus had called to them from the shoreline, telling them to try casting their nets again, that they might just catch some fish this time. And, boy, did they ever.

At the sight of this miracle, Peter dived right into the water and swam directly to Jesus, who was waiting for them around a charcoal fire, with fish and bread roasting for breakfast in the early-morning light. Does it sound like Jesus was there to berate him? To shame him? To fuel his sense of regret? To condemn Peter for being so unfaithful and disloyal? To tell him what would now be required of him to pay back the debt his sin had accumulated?

No, Jesus had already paid Peter's debt—and your debt, and my debt—days earlier when He died on the cross, and then rose from the dead. He'd forgiven Peter for denying Him, same as He's forgiven me for denying Him too. For though I'd slandered His name by living a life that neglected everything about what following Jesus truly means, He loved me, and called me into a relationship with Him. He forgave my years of thinking that head knowledge alone was sufficient for being saved from my sin. He changed my heart through His self-sacrificing love for me, and my whole life has been transformed by the power of the gospel.

I don't know where I'm catching you today. I don't know if you started following Jesus as a kid and sort of wandered away from Him. I don't know if you're even now still trying to straddle the two boats of a double life. I don't know if you're lashed with regret with no real idea for how to get past it, or maybe not so sure yet that you want to give up what you know to be wrong, even if it hurts on certain days and makes you feel ashamed.

All I really know is that I grew up in church. That was good. But it didn't make me good. Only through receiving Christ's righteousness and being given a new heart by God's grace could anything good ever come out of me. If He hadn't been pursuing me long before I was interested in running after Him, there'd be nothing worth telling of my story.

Today I'm still growing up in the church, learning more and more what it means to truly love Him, to grow even closer to Him. And I hope I'm still growing up in church from now until the day I die.

But this wasn't where my head (or heart) was located twenty years ago.

I still had a lot of growing up to do.

Chapter 3

Stuff Like This Doesn't Happen To Us

iddle-school Jamie loved God as much as she could. She did
M the right things and made some big commitments to herself,
to God, and to her parents. But looking back at middle-school
Jamie today, I'm quite certain those commitments she made were
motivated less by being true to her faith and more by how they
enabled her to fit in and be noticed by others. Being popular with
the cool kids, keeping up appearances, and getting praise from the
right people were what really drove her heart. So if committing
to keep herself pure made her stand out and get attention from
her peers and the adults in her life, then middle-school Jamie was
eager to do it.

But in high school, my stand for purity wasn't getting me
much attention anymore. Not many boys are lining up to date
girls who've committed not to kiss anybody until they're standing

at the altar with one. Holding to this stance is a bit drastic to a sixteen-year-old boy, unless you're sweet Stephen from Michigan. And Stephen's motor home caravan had long left Texas by this time. I was now back in the real world, trying to figure out how to do two things at once: stay pure for God while also getting the attention I craved.

And I was discovering these two things might not fit into the same heart.

Because, again, making the commitment not to kiss anyone was easy when I was convinced Stephen and I would one day smooch for the first time after we said, "I do." But the only reason this promise actually meant anything to me was because making it got me attention and praise from a guy. I think a clear sign that you're needing attention from boys is if you'd commit to never kissing one, just so a particular boy would like you.

And if I was willing to go *that* far, what else would I commit to doing for the attention and affection I might gain from my commitments?

It wasn't long until I found out.

Thinking back to this time in my life brings me so much sorrow—sorrow for the girl I became, sorrow for the children I'm raising. How I wish I'd known my worth to the Father during those years of my life, and how desperately I want my kids to know it themselves—how their Father in heaven adores them and has created them for grand purposes. My heart still aches for high-school Jamie, and for my own children, too, as they grow up and navigate these murky waters of wanting to be known and loved.

At the time, though, I was into making commitments . . . without truly knowing yet why I was making them.

My first big commitment after Stephen came as a freshman in high school when I signed my first True Love Waits card. If you didn't grow up around church in the 1990s, you might never have heard of True Love Waits. But it was a huge international initiative promoting sexual abstinence for teenagers and college students. All the church kids were doing it. Signing the cards, that is.

These calls for commitment were often made at a community-wide rally, if not on a Wednesday night at your local church's youth group time. (Side note again: if you didn't grow up a church kid, I'll do my best to explain our lingo.) "Youth group" is just what you'd think it is—a bunch of teenagers getting together in a structured environment at church. We met on Wednesday nights normally, where we sang for a while until our youth pastor (the staff member responsible for all the youth activities) got up and gave a little sermon. Then we mostly just hung out, which often meant girls on one side of the room and boys on the other, all hoping one day we'd be brave enough to mingle.

But back to True Love Waits and how it was presented at youth group night. Someone usually spoke to the students about the importance of saving yourself for marriage, and then they offered a time for teenagers to respond to this message—the chance to pledge yourself to a life of purity before you were married. (*True love waits,* see?) And to make your commitment official, they handed out pledge cards that said you were promising before God, as well as your family and friends, your future mate, even your future children, that you would keep yourself sexually abstinent until marriage. You signed the card, and you were good. Committed to the cause. Pledge made.

I believe there was even a True Love Waits day in Washington, DC, one year, where people came and placed their cards in the lawn and made a big hoopla about it. There were other big events, too, like where they stacked the cards to the top of a domed stadium. Several famous people were taking this stand publicly. It wasn't something that was only happening in my city. It was worldwide.

So I remember signing my pledge card that night. I even kept my copy in my Bible so that every time I opened it, usually on Sunday mornings and Wednesday nights, I could see this reminder—my pledge to keep myself pure until my wedding day.

The only problem with this pledge, for me, was that signing a card didn't make me feel any more loved and accepted than I'd felt before I signed it. Nothing changed in my heart. I'm not coming down on the True Love Waits plan, or any other similar program. Obviously, there's value in challenging believers to be true to God's teaching in Scripture. But I put my name on a piece of paper pledging to stay pure, though all the while my constant need for love and acceptance, my need for being known, was raging inside of my heart. All these things were fighting within me. And only one would win—either my pledge to be pure or my heart's longing for love.

Another commitment I made during my early teenage years was with my dad. He took me out one night to a super-nice dinner at the local Olive Garden, and I wore a dress my mom had made for me. Yes, there was a season that my mom made all of my dresses. I giggle about it now, but I actually loved it at the time! I got to pick out my own patterns and fabric—I was basically outsourcing my fashion needs to my mom! It was probably the same one she'd sewn for me to wear to my eighth-grade dance. Except I wasn't allowed to go to the eighth-grade dance—my parents weren't ready for their eighth-grade daughter to do the whole school dance thing! My friend Lindsey, who also wasn't allowed to go to the dance, and I got dates with our dads instead. A double date to a nice restaurant instead of the eighth-grade dance—practically every eighth-grade girl's dream, right?!?!?

But this wasn't that night. It was another night. And on this special date, when it was just him and me, he presented me with a necklace that had a key on it. I have no idea where my dad got this idea because he's not much the "idea kind of guy." Nonetheless, I was now the proud owner of a locket that I wore around my neck with a key on it. This key was to symbolize the key to my heart, and it was meant to stay with me until I was married, when I was supposed to present it to my husband on our wedding night. (Side note: Was I supposed to give him this key right *before* we had sex for the first time? I'm just gonna say that would be awkward. Or was I supposed to give it to him afterward? As some sort of prize? Even more awkward.)

Yet I was legitimately proud of this necklace and this moment. I truly felt loved by my dad, and I wanted desperately to please him. If only his love had been enough for my heart . . .

Unfortunately, however, I remember the day I broke all of these commitments.

At the time, it seemed as though breaking promises was the only cost of what I was doing—breaking my promise to my youth pastor, breaking my promise to my parents. Not until later did I understand the full weight of why these promises were so important. But in the moment, my commitment to keep myself pure until my wedding night didn't hold the same claim on my heart as everyone around me had hoped it would. That pledge card never stood a chance for me. It didn't make me feel loved, but this tangible boy in front of me did. The locket around my neck didn't make me feel treasured the way I desperately wanted to feel, but this boy did. He convinced me that I was a treasure to him.

He told me I was beautiful, that he loved me.

He said since we loved each other, this was something we could do together. A first for both of us.

It meant something.

It was special.

What we had was special.

We were in love.

In love. In love.

Weren't we?

No. As quickly as we fell "in love," *he* fell out of love. Just a summer romance for him, but the beginning of a long road for me—giving myself up in hopes of feeling loved in return. A road I would walk for years to come. A road that continued to define me even after I stopped walking it. A road that always left me feeling defeated and empty—unloved, unaccepted—the exact opposite of what I was looking for.

What started that summer before my junior year in high school became my norm for the next five years. And during those five years, I signed two more True Love Waits cards, filing them away in my Bible with the first one—each one a vivid reminder of what my youth pastor and parents wanted for me, although clearly I didn't understand what the big deal was. To me, at that time in my life, what I felt deep inside my heart from these other guys was real—as real as anything had ever been. I can roll my eyes now at high-school romance, at how incomplete that kind of love is, how fake and shallow it is. But as a sixteen-year-old girl, I was convinced I'd found my true love.

I was sure that's what my heart truly needed.

So, I continued the lifestyle of giving myself away to whoever would love me for that moment, all in hopes of feeling loved, desired, complete, and known—though always with the same result after every breakup of feeling unloved again, undesired again, incomplete again, unknown again.

All I wanted now was to feel those things again.

I love having people around my dinner table sharing a fabulous meal and enjoying each other's company. Something about a table full of delicious food brings everyone's guard down a bit, and often you'll get some raw and real experiences if you just ask the right questions.

I ask questions for a living on my podcast, *The Happy Hour*, but my interest in asking probing questions actually started on a cruise with some friends in 2010. I decided we needed to get the conversation moving around our table, so I facilitated some question-and-answer times. (Just call me cruise ship entertainer Jamie!)

I'm not sure I even remember where this question came from, but I've now asked it more times than I can count to guests around my dinner table at home. It's a simple question. Nothing too hard. No deep thinking needed. And the answer is only one word. Here's the question:

"Would you rather be *rich* or *famous*?"

That's it. See, I told you it was simple. But what I love about this question is that deep down, you aren't asking whether someone would rather be Warren Buffet, Oprah Winfrey, or Jennifer Aniston. You're actually just asking, "What drives you?" Is it riches? Recognition? Money? Is it fame? Neither one is better or worse than the other; they're just different. They both have their pitfalls, only different ones. "Would you rather be *rich* or *famous*?" That's the question that sparked our conversation on the cruise that night.

My friend Amy said *rich*.

Her husband, John, also said *rich*.

My brother, Jordan, and his wife, Kristen, both said *rich*.

Traci said *rich*, but her husband, Ryan, said *famous*.

What would you answer? Rich or famous?

Aaron's answer was *famous*, and so was mine. Still is today. Every time I'm asked, it's always the same. *Famous*. Again, I have no desire to be a movie star or a singer. (Actually, that's a lie. I would *love* to be a singer. Maybe like Carrie Underwood or Martina McBride or even Janet Jackson. If only I wasn't tone-deaf. I let that dream die a long time ago.) But I do desire greatly to be known.

I'm not particularly proud of this desire, but I can't deny it's always been there in my heart. For years, I filled that need with the love I received from boys. And even now, despite having the love of the only boy I ever need, this hole is still there sometimes. I realize the church answer is that *Jesus* fills that hole; He's the only one who matters—and this is indeed true. But we're human. And this hole seems to show up in my life more often than I would like to admit.

Instagram has confirmed this need in me. At first, I didn't really care how many likes or followers I was getting. No big deal. But then overnight it became a contest. A thousand followers . . . *five* thousand followers . . . *ten* thousand followers . . . goodness gracious, I now have *twenty-five* thousand followers. I'd better give them great pictures then. So they don't leave me. So that my number of followers doesn't start dropping.

So each picture now is crafted for *them*, not for me. No longer am I creating the family scrapbook I started out to make; now I'm creating the scrapbook my *followers* are demanding from me. Or at least that's what my heart keeps telling me.

To do whatever it takes. To be known.

My podcast has exposed this need in me as well. I still can't believe I just decided one day in May 2014 to start my own show. I also still can't believe there have been millions of downloads of my show since it started. Does this make me famous? Is this what I wanted? Is my goal each week to create a good show, or do I just want you to know who I am? Some days I'm not sure. The line gets super blurry for me sometimes.

To be known is the constant struggle of the darkest places in my soul. It's embarrassing to admit. But if I was being totally transparent with you, which I am, here's what I'd say:

> *Hi, my name is Jamie, and I have a super ugly place in my heart. I want to be known so badly that it's crippling sometimes. I thrive off of others' approval. I'm happy if you're happy with me, and I'm sad if you feel like I've let you down.*
>
> *Oh, and I also feel good when I'm known for something, and feel bad when I'm forgotten about something.*
>
> *Also, if you don't like me, I'm crushed. (Please say you like me. Please say I'm good at this podcasting, speaking, writing, at being a mother, a wife, a friend . . .)*

Is that not awful and exhausting? And yet so many of us live this way. The battle is constantly waging inside of us to be *known*, even though—without sounding too "churchy" here, I hope—in Jesus we are fully known and loved and accepted. Completely. He can truly satisfy the desires of our hearts, can satisfy each of our underlying needs. His love for us is beyond our understanding, and yet right in front of us all the time.

In fact, let me tell you how far beyond my understanding Jesus' love has become for me. He knows I'm a sinner. He is fully aware of my struggle and desire for being known and loved. His desire is also freedom for me. He knows that my only source for being loved and known is in Him, and in His great kindness, He has given me a job that constantly puts me in front of people. In His kindness toward me, He brings this struggle to the surface, so that it can be dealt with and not left to destroy me. My job depends on more people knowing who I am. It's almost like He wrote me a letter that says:

> *Jamie, I know your greatest desire, as well as your greatest weakness. So I'm going to throw you into the game with a job that depends on being known. From inside this job— where you'll be constantly tempted to seek your satisfaction in the love and acceptance of other people—this is how I'll best be able to show you that you constantly need Me, can constantly come back to Me, and can constantly remember that only in Me are you truly known.*

*Now, go make your podcast, go stand on stages to speak,
and go write a book pouring out your soul. Have fun. And
along the way, let's get you free from needing others to make
you feel good about yourself. All you need is Me.*

I love you . . .

Can you think of a similar example of this in your own life?
Where God is tossing you into the deep end of your greatest need,
for the purpose of showing You in the process that He is all you'll
ever need?

Isn't that just so strong and beautiful of Him?

For years, I laughed about my desire to be famous versus rich.
And if you ask me today, my answer will still be the same. But
I'm not so flippant about it anymore. I realize I'm fighting this
sin on a daily basis of finding love and acceptance in other places
and people besides God. Some days I have it beat; other days it
takes me out all over again. But every day, no matter my level of
fight, He is always there pursuing me, loving me, forgiving me,
and reminding me of the efforts He went to in order to make me
His child.

But I know deep down where my desire comes from. It's from
wanting to be truly known and loved for exactly who I am. And
that's something I've discovered can only come from God.

Throughout those years, I tried getting it met in other places, searching for something that no person could ever give me. Although sex is a precious gift from God, intended to help us become intimately known by another person—by *one* person, in marriage—I was using it with all the wrong people, at all the wrong times. That's why it could never come close to satisfying my innermost desires. It always fell short of giving me what I needed. It always left me with that empty feeling you get, after you've placed your hope in something that fails you every single time.

Every. Single. Time.

Looking back on my teenage years, I remember how many times I vowed to never drink again and never have sex again. Usually these promises to God followed an evening that held much regret, or a morning where memories were hard to recall. Nonetheless, my promises only lasted until the next drink was offered, or until the next date night. In my head the life I was living was no different from the life everyone else I knew was living. What was the big deal anyway? I was a big girl who could handle my big-girl choices.

A few months ago, I was laid up sick on the couch and decided to watch some TV from those younger days. *Friends* was on, and so of course I had to stop and watch Rachel, Ross, Monica, and the whole gang. Several segments in the show made me pause as I was watching. The flippant way that sex was talked about and portrayed on the show is exactly how I was living in my late teenage years. In fact, not having sex with someone I was dating seemed odd to me. Weird. I had never yet been in a relationship where dating didn't equate to sex. That was completely normal to me—despite how obviously messed-up this kind of thinking is. I knew my parents would be so angry and disappointed if they found out. I would die if my grandma knew this part of my life.

Yet this was who I was, and I felt little need to change. And even when I did—even in those moments when I felt guilty or wanted to be different—I didn't know how to stop. How do you just wake up one day and decide you don't want to have sex any-more, especially when nothing else makes you feel loved, accepted, and wanted like that? The only way I could stop living that way was if Jesus intervened. And I couldn't see how anything He might give me could compare to what my heart felt from being with my boyfriend.

Deep in my soul I reassured myself that what I was doing was okay. After all, I was hardly the worst girl in school. Besides, I didn't sleep with *lots* of guys, only the guy I was dating (as if that noble distinction was something I should be proud of). So, in my mind, I was still a good girl—a good churchgoing girl—who was doing normal things that everyone else was doing. I wasn't doing drugs. I wasn't sleeping around recklessly. I was making good grades, and—hey, I even had a job at a daycare loving on kids. Takes only a good girl to do that, doesn't it?

And yet I would give myself away to whoever would love me.

That was high-school Jamie.

And, um . . . well . . .

College Jamie too.

I'd done the best I could to shield my unsavory social habits from my parents, but you can never do it completely. So while I assumed my parents were completely clueless to my reckless ways, they might have been on to me more than I thought. One indicator of this was that they sent me to a private Christian college in Dallas, in hopes that I would get myself together.

The thing about immersing someone into a certain environment, and putting all of your hope in that place to help them get their life together, is that it is never enough. No place, person, or event on its own can get someone's life back on track. The only thing that can change someone's life is a surrendered relationship with Jesus. Remember, I knew all about God and could say all the right things, but there was no intimacy between God and me. I kept looking all around me at college for intimacy, love, and affection, for that feeling of being known, even while God was continually pursuing me, offering me the joy of having all my needs met in Him.

I've heard it said that college is when you find out who you really are. In most cases, you're heading to a new place where people don't already know you. So, in a weird way, you can entirely re-create yourself, your image, your identity. But for me, I didn't really try re-creating much of myself at all—except that I stopped even trying to be the "good Christian girl" on the outside. I became exactly the girl I wanted to be. The real Jamie showed up at college—not the girl who grew up in the church, who believed in God, who would choose Jesus over any counterfeit savior, and who for the most part lived an honorable life. I still didn't do drugs, still didn't smoke cigarettes. I clung to those things as sort of a measuring stick for how far I would go in life. No drugs. No cigarettes. But anything else, I was game for.

My first day on campus, I met two guys who were on the baseball team. I'm not saying baseball players can't love Jesus; I'm saying at a private Christian school, most of the athletes could not care less about their faith. They only came to this particular school because it's where they got a scholarship.

So, I'd found my people for the next two years. We partied hard. Most of the time we even showed up to class. My sweet roommate, who loved Jesus and was saving herself for marriage, looked down on me for not coming home some nights. She knew

I was physically safe, just that I'd decided to sleep wherever the party had ended for the night.

Looking back on that time and the careless life I lived—how embarrassing—a miracle I didn't end up dead or with a disease. There are so many things I'm ashamed of in my life. So many. Countless moments I wish I could change or do over. And my first two years of college are rather high on that "do over" list. I'm not saying I didn't have fun. Big fun. But I was losing myself. I would literally wake up and not know what had happened the night before. I would go to class in someone's T-shirt from whatever house I'd stayed at.

But my lifestyle of partying was about to catch up to me, and it was going to catch up hard.

Spring semester, sophomore year.

I found myself in a situation that wasn't entirely new to me—something that had happened before and had always cleared itself up. *I was late with my period.* But I was sure it would work out fine again.

I'd shed many tears in high school over the what-ifs of being late. You'd think these close encounters would have affected my decision to continue having unprotected sex. I just always thought that something like this would surely never happen to me. That's what happens to *those* girls. Not me.

But it wasn't one of those times where it worked out fine.

I was one of those girls now.

She was me.

And as stupid as it sounds, this wasn't even a long-term boy-friend. I'd only been dating this guy for a few months. Had never met his parents. Didn't even know his middle name. Yet here I was—indeed pregnant—at twenty years old with a guy who was still a relative stranger to me.

I guess there's no need to try describing how devastating this new development was. I couldn't believe it. Stuff like this wasn't supposed to happen to college Jamie. I may not have been living the life of the good Christian girl, but I thought I was a Christian girl just the same. A "grew up in the church" girl. A Bible Drill and youth group girl.

And yet when the initial shock died down, I was rather surprised how quickly my can-do, make-do spirit kicked into gear. I convinced myself I could make this work. I'd be fine. I moved into his apartment, hung my pictures on the wall, found my drawers in the dresser, put my toothbrush in the bathroom, and we began playing house. We were going to be a family. The best thing to do, I figured, was to marry this man. I mean, surely I loved him enough to become his wife. Right? I mean, I was pregnant with his child. Can you do that and not truly love somebody? And not be truly loved in return?

For a few weeks of naïve denial, I tried to forget what was going on. I pushed it out of mind. I mean, I looked the same. Felt the same. Everybody was still treating me the same. But pretty soon, I could no longer deny the fact that I needed to have the hardest conversation I'd ever had with anybody in my life.

I had to tell my parents.

Obviously, this chore would be difficult in *any* situation. But I knew when I revealed this news to my parents, I wouldn't just be telling them about my pregnancy. My confession would also be wrapped up in all the failed commitments I'd made since I was their middle-school Jamie. The locket hadn't worked; the True Love Waits cards hadn't worked; the special dates with my dad hadn't worked. Nothing had worked. None of those things had kept me pure. I had broken all my commitments a long time ago, and now I'd only be filling in my mom and dad on the disaster of a life I'd created for myself.

And I wasn't sure how to do that. I had no idea what to expect. I had let them down big-time, and they were sure to freak out. The only bright side was that there was a baby involved in this con-versation—*guess what, y'all, you're going to be grandparents!* Maybe whatever anger they felt and expressed would be tempered by that.

Still, I couldn't be sure. So I opted for a public place. I'm no dummy. I wasn't about to drive to their *house* to tell them, where I'd be stuck, unable to escape whatever emotions might spill out.

Then further modifying my plan, I decided to tell only my dad first. He was the less likely of the two to lose his mind with me. I even figured out just how to do it. My brother was running at a track meet in Waco, so I made the drive down alone from Dallas to watch him run. I didn't bring my baby daddy along, just me. I sat with my dad and some other parents during the meet, cheering my brother on as he ran, all the while knowing I was holding a bomb inside that would soon ignite when I told my dad of my impending marriage and motherhood.

I'd decided that right before it was time to part ways, I would tell him. The last-minute words wouldn't leave him much time to process it all and overreact. (I told you I was no dummy.) Although I don't recall exactly how I told him, I vaguely remember it going something like this:

> ME: Sure been great to see you, Dad.
>
> DAD: You too, Jamie, thanks for driving down. I know your brother appreciates it.
>
> ME: Yeah, no big deal! I love watching him run.
>
> DAD: Great. Well, we'll see you in a few weeks.
>
> ME: Sounds great! Oh—by the way, Dad, I'm pregnant.
>
> DAD: What?
>
> ME: Yeah. You've never met the guy, but . . . he's great.

DAD: What?

ME: I think we're going to get married this summer.

DAD: What?

For real, that happened. Which left my dad rather shocked and a bit taken aback by the conversation. (No kidding, right?) And though my plan had called for him to be the one who went home and told my mom, he made it quite clear that I would need to be the one to tell her myself. Which is what I was afraid he would say. I was a big girl now, making big-girl choices—like getting pregnant and all—so the least I could do was call my mom on the phone and let her know she was going to be a grandma!

Needless to say, the phone call didn't go well. My mom was, uh . . . let's go with *furious* . . . though not nearly as furious at me for being pregnant as she was furious that I was even entertaining the idea of marrying this guy. My mom well knew the old saying that two wrongs don't make a right. I sure didn't need to make another mistake, she said, of marrying a guy I hardly knew, just to make up for the mistake of having sex with him before I was married.

From the clear hindsight of time, I'm beyond thankful for her insightful anger on this issue, and I'd like to say I trusted her and followed her lead on it.

But I didn't. My boyfriend and I continued playing house. I worked; he worked; we talked about a wedding day, baby names, all the things you do when preparing to become a mom and a wife all in the same year.

And then all of it shattered. The whole dream—unsound and accidental though it was—fell apart.

I was at the apartment one day when I noticed the blood. For a twenty-year-old who'd never been pregnant—in fact, had never known anyone up close who'd been pregnant—this was scary. I called my doctor, and the lady on the phone told me not to worry. It *could* be bad, but it could just as easily be normal. Only time would tell. We set in for the wait.

The thing about being twenty and unexpectedly pregnant is that, at first, it's the worst thing in the world that could ever happen to you, and then it becomes the greatest. Of course, I didn't plan my life this way, and of course I didn't desire to be a teenage mom. But here I was. What could I do about it? I never entertained the idea of abortion, so my next option was to pick myself up and carry on. I would be a momma. And as soon as you make that choice, you're in love with the baby in your belly, and all the other variables don't seem to be that big of a deal anymore.

But now this blood was threatening this baby. And we were still waiting to see if it was okay blood or bad blood.

It looked bad. Even with resting and staying off my feet, I started bleeding more, and we decided to go to the ER to get this whole situation checked out. Hand in hand we walked in, both in love with this baby, and honestly not much in love with each other. How *could* we be? We hardly knew each other. Our baby had become the glue between us, and we were feeling as though the glue was slowly unsticking. A few weeks before, we'd planned on keeping this baby and getting married before he or she was born. Now we found ourselves in the ER in the middle of the night, and I was feeling as though everything was falling apart. Things didn't seem as they were supposed to seem. As much as I had never planned to be a mom at twenty, this baby I loved was in jeopardy, and I was a mess.

As long as I live, I'll never forget what transpired next. The doctor walked in, looked me straight in the eyes, and—no joke, he said it just like this: "Yep, the baby's dead." How could anybody say something as heartless and matter-of-fact as that? I know we were two barely past teenagers with zero clues about life, but we loved this baby, and his words hurt me to the core. It was the most awful interaction I've ever had with a doctor in my entire life.

Now the glue between my boyfriend and me was indeed gone. I walked into that hospital a momma, and I left a twenty-year-old lost girl—a girl who thought she'd found a man and a baby to fill all the holes in her life, who thought she was about to be known and loved in a grand way.

Now what would I/we do?

We continued to play house, but it didn't feel right to me anymore. I didn't love this man enough to spend forever with him without our child. The baby was why I'd chosen forever with him, and now that there was no baby, I decided there would be no forever between *us* either. Honestly, I think he knew this too. We weren't in love, and it was evident. We were two kids who got ourselves in a situation, and we thought we could make it right with a ceremony and wedding bands. But now there was no need for all that hoopla. We were done.

The emotions of losing something you loved but never wanted in the first place are exhausting. At first I was devastated by the loss of my child. I was beyond sad and wanted everything back like it was before. The tears flowed endlessly, and I couldn't seem to function again because of the sadness that had overcome me.

Then a few weeks later, I began to feel relieved. Relieved that I wasn't becoming a mom before I'd planned for this responsibility. Relieved that I could finish school without the setback a baby would create for me. Then guilt rushed over me for feeling relieved. How could I feel relieved from losing a child? Sorrow. Relief. Guilt. A constant wave of emotions.

Finally, I asked my parents if I could move back home. I knew I couldn't process these emotions in Dallas. I needed a safe place to land . . . because the pregnancy, as tough as it was, hadn't been rock bottom for me. The miscarriage was what took me to rock bottom. The pregnancy was a hurdle we would jump, and life would continue on. The miscarriage left me feeling more alone than ever before. And for the first time in a really long time, I felt as though there just might be more to life than the way I'd been living. What if the church stuff I followed in middle school was right? What if I was worth more than this? What if God actually did have big plans for me? But even if those things were true, how could they still be true for me now?

I moved home in the summer of 1998, and had never been more alone in my entire life.

Chapter 4

Chased by God

The year was 1998. This was the summer I attached the first pin to my chest. Up until then, I never knew about all the pins I should be wearing.

Funny, isn't it, that it wasn't until I moved home and started going to church again that I felt the need to do this pin-attaching thing. The one place where I was supposed to feel the most freedom—at church—actually produced the most shame in me. I'm not saying the people there were looking down on me. Maybe they were; maybe they weren't. Or maybe I was just so convinced they *should* look down on me that I created a world in my mind where they *did* look down on me. I don't know.

Nevertheless, these letters began to make their home on my chest.

"U" for *used*.

"W" for *whore*.

"P" for *pregnant*.

"S" for *shame*.

Worse, these labels also began to become my identity and make their home in my heart. I believed I was *all* of those things. And if I was all of those things, then I had no right going to church and acting as if I wasn't. My feelings about myself, symbolized by those pins and letters, formed my new identity. And I would acquire more pins along the way.

I didn't know any other way to be identified. If you're not a follower of Christ, how else *can* you be identified, except by the choices you've made, the things you've said, the places you've been. Not until God steps into our world and literally gives us a new identity can we be anything other than the life we've decided to live. As sinners. Unrepentant sinners.

But I didn't believe this new identity could happen to me. If it already had, I couldn't tell. And even if it still could, I surely didn't deserve it now.

That's how I was thinking.

That's what brought on the pins.

Church in my mind at that time was still the place for people who already had their stuff together. I had no concept of church as a place where broken people could show up, be their real selves, and still receive love. If ever I'd tried to actually be myself at church, I felt I would've been asked not to come back. If they knew the real me, they would suggest other places for me to go. Because despite having been raised in the church, I really had no working concept of the gospel, the forgiveness of Christ, and God's love for me. In my mind, you were either a good person and God loved you, or you were a bad person and God didn't love you. I loved God as much as I knew how, but I was certain His love for me had been slowly fading through the years. And if I didn't get my act together quickly, He would quit loving me altogether. I felt that I had strung Him along for way too long. Yet I had no concept of how to get started again. I felt so lost—even at home. Lost—even at church. Everyone wanted me to be different. I did too. But how?

Now, just for a moment, before going any further, I want to pull back from this scene, in order to say that this same dynamic I experienced is playing out this week, this weekend, everywhere that people and churches exist. And wherever it does, you and I are on either side of it. We're either the church people that others feel too ashamed to be themselves around, or we're the bottled-up people whose sense of failure or inadequacy makes us want to hide and maybe *hate* you.

Do you see the problem with this picture? Do you see the needless anxiety and waste of time we cause for others and ourselves when church is a place where people feel unwelcome to be real?

I realize, of course, sin causes separation. Sin must be dealt with. No one is helped by being coddled and petted in their sin, practically encouraged not to sweat what it does to all of us. But everything should be pointing to Jesus. Our churches should do nothing else but point people to Jesus, the true Redeemer of their souls. We can't be giving off the vibe that says certain people don't quite measure up. (Because that's not true.) And if we're the ones who *feel* like we don't measure up, we can't be beating ourselves to death for things that Christ has already taken the blows for. (Which actually *is* true.)

I'll come back to this subject later, throughout this whole journey we're taking together, because its implications are so important. But whether my story is *unlike* yours and you're not sure what to make of rebel kids like me, or whether my story is all too *similar* to yours and you're not sure what to do next, I'm praying that the experiences still to be shared in these remaining chapters will cause you to truly feel for the ashamed . . . and, if you're the ashamed, will cause you to run toward freedom whatever it costs.

Because, get this straight—God is running to you.

Even if you're sitting at rock bottom.

Something weird happens to you when you hit rock bottom. Your only view is what's above you. Rock bottom is lonely. Rock bottom is scary. For me, rock bottom was an opportunity to reevaluate life as I knew it. My parents were gracious toward me and patient in my journey. They never made me go to church with them but, then again, it's just what I always did. Going to church on Sundays at home was as normal as my family going to Grandma's for Christmas. It's just what we did.

But the funny thing about church for someone who feels as though they've hit rock bottom is that church can sometimes make you feel anxious. In your brain you feel as though everyone is on to you. They know your junk, and even if you were to try hiding it, you can't, because they all know. It feels as if they had a big meeting before the doors opened, and everyone was clued in on your sin struggles. Of course, we all know church is nothing like that (or at least isn't supposed to be like that), but for someone like me who was walking around with a big secret—with all those pins—this was my perceived reality.

This was exactly how I felt. I would protect myself and my heart at all costs, even from these church people. *Especially* from these church people.

But here's when—looking back at least, even if not at the time—I started to suspect that something else, something highly unusual, was going on. Because even though church made me feel terrible, I spent that summer trying so hard to get involved in the college ministry.

Why? What was I doing? Why was I putting myself through this?

I didn't even like them, the college kids at our church. They were so *unlike me*. I mean, if they were attending church, surely they weren't doing anything wrong. None of them had likely been pregnant just last month, for instance. Or were mourning the loss of an unborn child that no one knew about. Or probably had ever tasted alcohol in their whole lives. None of them had ever walked in my shoes. None of them were living with a secret as big as mine. None of them knew what it was like to hurt—to *really* hurt—to make poor choices, to feel as alone as I was feeling.

Twenty years removed from this time in my life, I realize the reason why I made all these assumptions of them was because I was too afraid to tell anyone about myself. If I had, I might have found they'd walked through some hard stuff too. But I was so inwardly focused on my own pain and hurts that I didn't look around to see others who were also in pain. All I saw were a bunch of goody-two-shoes who wanted nothing to do with me, who couldn't relate to me, who didn't care about me. I felt unaccepted by them before they even had a chance to ask my name. I felt left out, ignored, frowned upon, less-than, and didn't really give them a chance to show me otherwise. And if those college girls couldn't love me for who I was, then how could God love me? That's how skewed my thoughts had become. I put *their* ideas of me (or at least my *perceived* ideas of their ideas) above *God's* ideas about me.

From their side, I'm certain they felt *I* was the rude one—stand-offish, probably a little stuck up—when, in fact, the exact opposite was true. I was scared of letting anyone into my life for fear of their judgment, of their lack of love, of their possibly telling me what I believed to be true—that I was indeed unlovable. I feared that if I let them in on my world, they would reject me. So to protect myself, I put up a guard. No one was getting in that might hurt me, even if they were trying to love me.

I went from being someone desperate to be *known* to someone whose main desire was to stay *unknown.*

And yet I kept coming in—for reasons I didn't even know or want. This was so weird. And so hard. But what I didn't know until later was that God was amazingly at work. He was already beginning the process of bringing my secrets out from under wraps so He could bring my freedom into real life.

He was making my path back to Him . . . unavoidable.

By fall, I started back to school, this time locally in Houston. I knew I needed to get back into life, with a plan, though I honestly wasn't sure what that even looked like. I'd spent the summer working for my dad's company, hanging out with my family, and wondering if I would ever get back to a normal life again. In the past three months, I'd been pregnant, preparing to get married, dealing with a miscarriage, moving back home, and now living with a secret over my head. What would this mess look like if it went back to school now?

The only way I knew to make college better this time was to be a better person. I would stop getting drunk. I would stop having sex. I would start reading my Bible. Wouldn't that make me feel better about myself? Wouldn't that make God love me? Wouldn't that make me feel like a good person?

So that became my goal: Stop getting drunk. Stop having sex. God would love me then, and I would be acceptable to Him again. *Loved. Accepted.* That was still what I wanted. And maybe at twenty years old, being good would finally do it for me.

But the problem with behavior modification is that it never sustains the test of time. Doing good things to be a better person can never satisfy the desires of your heart. We always fail. We always let God down. We never become good enough.

And not having sex was just behavior modification for me. It had nothing to do with saving myself for marriage because of my love for God; it had everything to do with trying so hard to do the right thing so that God would love me, and so that I wouldn't get pregnant again.

So I entered the fall semester trying to do life better. And I tried really hard.

For about two weeks!

Probably didn't help that I joined a sorority before school even started. Nothing against the Greek system, but it's a super hard place to try and do "good things" like not drink and not have sex. In fact, as I began to embrace sorority life, I became the stereotypical sorority girl. Drunk and easy. Once again, I was failing at the "being good" challenge I had given myself. But for someone who's immersed in a lifestyle, it's hard to do anything other than what you already know. And for me, I still didn't know how to date without sex being involved. I'd been doing it that way since I was sixteen. I didn't believe a guy loved me unless he wanted to go to bed with me, and I saw nothing wrong with a first date ending in a sleepover.

So even with my big commitment again to be this good girl that I thought I needed to be for God to love me and for the people at church to accept me, I kept failing. All I knew how to be was the girl I'd been for the past four years. Becoming someone else was hard. Maybe impossible. It was an act I didn't know how to keep up. I only knew how to be me, and the good-girl act wasn't me. She was fake.

Halfway through that fall semester, I met a guy who became my boyfriend—the first guy I'd seriously dated since the miscarriage.

I wasn't living like I should, I knew, but at least I had *this* exciting relationship to be part of. He wasn't a Christian, but I thought it would be fine. I mean, we were both good people.

But, boy, did it turn out to be a different experience than all the other times I'd been involved with a guy. Because while God had been pursuing me for the past few years, I was most unaware of His pursuit, but the next twelve months of my life would make it obvious that He was there. He had always been there, and He was about to flip my world completely upside down.

You may or may not understand what I'm about to say. But being pursued by God was the scariest thing in my life. *Really? Scarier than being a pregnant teenager? Scarier than the doctor delivering the news that your baby was dead?* Yes. Partly because He would eventually lead me to a point of unavoidable vulnerability that felt more crippling to me than anything I'd ever been through before. And partly because I felt like if He rejected me, the way I thought other people would reject me, I would truly have nothing. To be rejected and abandoned, rather than loved and accepted, wasn't something I thought I could live with. And that's what I was afraid of—if God ever really got hold of me—that He would reject me.

But there's really no other reasonable explanation for what happened next in my life except that God just did it, that He was chasing me down, and that He wasn't going to stop until He'd caught me. I look back at this time, and I see the hand of God all over it. Things I would normally scoff at, I was agreeing to participate in. Things I would never care about were actually keeping me up at night, thinking about them.

Places I would never go, and people I would never want to spend this much time with, were about to change my life forever.

Somehow I was invited to attend a conference in Dallas with the college ministry at our church (the college kids that I hated so much). We were to drive up from Houston, stay in a hotel together, and go all weekend to this big event. Fun, huh? No, not to me.

Then why, again, was I saying YES to this idea? Agreeing to hang out for a whole weekend with people I couldn't stand? A weekend that was all about this God who was doing crazy things in me, all while I was scared to death of not being good enough for Him?

It just didn't make sense.

Yet I knew I needed to go.

And so I went. I even signed up to share a ride, which ended up putting me with a girl named Erica (who I actually wish I'd gotten to know better because I think we were both living the same double life) and this guy named Aaron.

Aaron Ivey.

We already knew each other a little bit. A month earlier, in fact, he had asked me on a date. Can you believe that? But I'd recently started dating my current boyfriend, so I politely refused.

Sweet of him, though—one of those perfectly put-together college kids, thinking he could mix it up with somebody like me. He had no idea what he was asking. He and I would never work.

But we did venture up to this conference together—Passion Conference, it was called. I remember only two things from that entire weekend. First, I remember this Aaron guy was hilarious. I'd been wrong about him. He was different from the other college kids that, at least from my perception, couldn't wrap their minds around somebody like me. He seemed authentic and real. I didn't feel as though he looked down on me, even though I was certain if he knew the real me, he would change his mind and get away from me as fast as he could. Yet for the first time since doing anything with these kids from the college ministry, this person made me feel safe. He made church and me feel *safe* together.

The second thing I remember was that something truly remarkable happened to me during that event. I can't make it splashy in trying to describe it because it wasn't something noticeable, I don't think, to others. I wasn't even sure I understood it myself. I just knew it was happening. And I knew it was real.

God wooed me to Himself that weekend.

For the first time ever, I felt *known* by Him, and yet *loved* by Him, all at the same time—not because I was doing something right or was on one of my good-girl kicks, but because He just loved me.

I'm sure we sang worship songs while we were there, but I don't really have any recollection of them—nor of the place where we stayed, the restaurants where we ate, or who was sitting next to me at each session. I only remember a woman named Beth Moore (who I'd never heard of) standing on the stage and saying words that struck me as if she'd come there to say them only to me. I'd never felt God luring me toward Him like that, tugging at my heart like that. He was speaking, and I heard Him—really heard what was on His heart—for the first time in my life.

Incredibly, I've been honored to interview Beth on my podcast. (It sounds so crazy now, as I think back to the first time I saw her, and what my life was like at the time.) Being able to tell her in person how the Holy Spirit penetrated my heart that day and about the unexpected, unexplainable joy He brought to me in that moment is still one of my lifetime favorite moments.

But that's exactly how it happened. There at a Christian conference, which was so not my thing, I found myself being drawn to Christ in such an unlikely way. I truly felt broken for my sin and I knew that Jesus—not my attempt at keeping His rules and expectations, but Jesus Himself—was the something that was missing from my life. I believe that I was experiencing a godly grief for the first time in my life. I'd always known His story and what He'd done, from having grown up in the church. But finally, I understood what His sacrifice on the cross, and resurrection from the dead truly meant for me. For the first time, I felt as though the church—which had lately been a place where I only felt shame— might actually have a place for me and my brokenness.

God had chased me down.

And changed me forever.

I love seeing Jesus interact with women in the Bible, how He loved, pursued, and included them in His ministry. I told Aaron recently that my next book would be called *Jesus and His Ladies*. Catchy, I think, but . . . probably open to misinterpretation.

Yet the story in John 4 of Jesus' encounter with the woman at the well is a picture of Him meeting a woman right where she was. Literally and figuratively.

Most Jewish travelers of that day made a point of avoiding the region of Samaria. The history between the Jews and the Samaritans was a bit rocky, and so to prevent unwanted interaction with them, they would walk completely out of their way. Jesus, however, went there on purpose. To meet *those* people.

Goodness gracious, do I know what it feels like to be one of "those people." I've felt like an outsider a few times in my life, and I can tell you this: you never expect an insider to join you on the outside. This woman at the well was an outsider; Jesus was an insider. Yet He entered her world—He came *to her*—creating an interaction that not even *she* wanted to happen.

Their conversation at first was a bit awkward and uncomfortable. You probably know the story. Jesus said to her, "Give me a drink," and instead of offering Him a drink, she basically said to Him, "Why are YOU, a Jew, talking to ME, a Samaritan woman?"

I felt this exact way when Jesus started pressing closer to me. I would wonder to myself, *Why in the world does He want anything to do with me?* I knew the fraud that I was. I knew the way I'd trampled His name and His reputation into the ground with my words and actions.

Have you ever felt this way before, when thinking about your relationship with God? How in the world could He love *you*? How could He want to be in a relationship with *you*? How could He possibly use *you* . . . the way *you* are? Know what I'm talking about?

Those were actually some of the same thoughts that prohibited me from following Jesus for so long. I truly didn't think a girl like me could be loved by a God like Him. I had been given too many chances to turn my life around and I had rejected them all, so surely God would do the same to me. Rejection was the only option I could conceive in my mind. I had rejected *Him*, so therefore He would reject *me* . . . except for the fact that He is Jesus, and Jesus doesn't do rejection. He pursues hearts.

In the case of this woman, if Jesus had wanted to do rejection, she was already holding all the ingredients for it. Five former husbands. Living with a man who wasn't her husband. Now standing next to a Man who in reality was her Creator, the God of the universe. Do you see a rejection scenario setting up here?

But He wasn't there to reject her. He was there to pursue her heart, to provide her with water that would satisfy her forever—a concept that must have blown her mind because she was so thirsty that she went for it. "Sir, give me this water, so that I will not be thirsty or have to come here to draw water" (John 4:15).

Ahh, that's so beautiful. Jesus was the only thing that could quench her desire for being known, loved, and accepted as she was. He was the only one who could satisfy her so much that she would no longer need to venture out to this well at odd hours, times when other women wouldn't be around so she could avoid the embarrassment, shame, and horror of them knowing her junk, cutting eyes at her, whispering behind her back . . . rejecting her.

Jesus came to free her, not to condemn her.

Her biggest sin wasn't her five husbands and all the other junk we know of her from Scripture. Her biggest sin was unbelief. And that's what Jesus came to deal with. To offer her "living water." He is more concerned with drawing our hearts toward Him, not getting us put together enough so that we're *capable* of coming to Him. The reason He wants us acknowledging and repenting of our sins is so that we can follow Him, not so He can confirm why He's rejecting us. "For God did not send his Son into the world to condemn the world, but in order that the world might be saved through him" (John 3:17).

If you aren't a follower of Jesus, know that He isn't asking you to get your life together before you follow Him. He wants us to follow Him, worship Him, and give Him our all. And when we do that, our life does start to get together. Our picture of this is pretty much all wrong—that we need be perfected before we come to God. In reality, the exact opposite is true. He does the perfecting in us the more we come to know Him.

He doesn't chase us just to catch us. He chases us so we can follow Him.

The woman at the well was me. I was the one hiding at the well while the other women were at home. I was the woman at home while the other women were at the well. I was one that Jesus knew so much about, yet He still chose to love me, pursue me, and want to be in a relationship with me.

For the first time in my life, I felt *known*. And even if it wasn't exactly what I wanted to be known for, I discovered it's what we're *all* known for, or should *want* to be known for.

Known for needing Jesus.

My experience at the Passion Conference truly changed me. But I wasn't sure what to do with this change. I knew I couldn't be a Christian and live the way I was living. But I didn't know if I could live how I thought Christians lived. To me, they were boring, judgmental, too good for me, no fun. How could I give my super-fun life over to *that*? Was this what Jesus wanted of me now?

A few months later, I signed up to go on a ski trip with our church. My dad and brother were both going, and so it made sense for me to join them as well. The church rented a bus, and we traveled the grueling journey from Houston to Breckenridge, Colorado—and lo and behold, I ended up sitting next to that same guy from the Passion trip again. (Remember the guy who's now my husband?!) Aaron and I had so much fun on that trip. We ended up skiing together a lot. I still don't think I've ever laughed so much. Aaron was really fun to be around, and it might have been the first time in my life I was having fun with a guy who I wasn't trying to entice sexually.

We were merely friends. He was that funny guy from church who sang on the stage during worship services. He was my brother's youth pastor. But that was it. And that was enough. And it felt nice for me and another guy to just be friends. For that to be enough.

The best thing about this story is to hear Aaron tell it. He claims we frolicked in the mountains laughing and falling in love together, but in reality, he was the only one falling in love, not me. We did have fun, yes, but he was just a friend. In fact, when we arrived back in Houston, my boyfriend picked me up from the church parking lot. My fun, easygoing week in the slopes with one of the nicest guys I'd ever met was over. But as proof of what God was doing, the contrast that was forming between Aaron and my boyfriend—between my old life and my new one—would soon force me to make a monumental choice.

It was like I was now on two tracks, the life I was so used to living and this new life following God. And though the track that God was calling me toward was something I wanted—the life of following Him that He was calling me to choose—the other track didn't just automatically merge with the new one. Other people were still on it with me. I was still in the middle of living there. So even in the midst of all this change in my heart toward God, my relationship with the guy I was dating continued to progress. And before I knew it, we were engaged and planning a wedding, all while moving along on two separate tracks, hoping they would eventually merge together.

I know you are wondering how this will work out. My life was radically changed at Passion, and now I'm engaged to someone who isn't even a Christian. He was starting to come to church with me. That was good. Sort of fit with the life I was wanting to start living now. I was moving toward becoming a married woman, with a husband who sat there with me on Sundays and sang the songs and listened to the sermon. That's how this was all going to come together, right? We're all Christians, right? We're Americans. We're Texans.

Christians.

But, no, it still wasn't exactly right. We were still having sex, for instance. Which didn't seem to bother *him* but . . . like on that summer day around my sixteenth birthday when I'd had sex for the first time ever, it was really bothering *me*.

Over the years, as my conscience wore down, sex in a relationship had become such a no-brainer. Being in a relationship and not having sex would've seemed weird and odd. (I hate saying it, but it was true.) But now, all of a sudden, I was starting to feel incredibly guilty about it. Remember the godly grief I mentioned before? Here is a prime example of this newfound guilt in my life—it led me to repentance. I mean, here I was, progressing toward a wedding date with this man, and yet already drifting apart from him. He didn't share the same newfound principles and love for Jesus that I was beginning to crave. We weren't on this faith journey of mine together. It was just me, even if he'd temporarily been willing to add a Sunday-morning interruption to his weekend schedule.

But the hypocrisy, for me, had to stop. Jesus was pursuing me, wanting me to follow Him. And that meant following Him in everything.

I finally developed the courage to express my convictions on this subject to my fiancé. And it didn't go quite as I had expected. I was naïve enough to think that he actually loved me for who I was, not only for what we shared in the bedroom. Sure, I expected him to be a little bummed to be missing out on sex, but—hey, we were soon to be married. Wouldn't be like this forever. Surely he would still love me just the same. And would wait, for a change.

Except that's not what happened. He couldn't fathom my decision. And to pile on—to make it look like I was the one who should be ashamed here—he threw my past pregnancy in my face, and told me how mean I was being to him to force this kind of change on him so quickly.

Can we say, red flags waving everywhere?!?

What was I gonna do? My devotion to God was real, but it was shaky. And it was now causing a big source of tension between us. I was willing to give this "following Jesus" thing a try, but what if it cost me my relationship? And yet I was genuinely growing to love God more than ever, and able to get over my boyfriend's frustration with me less.

I'll never forget the day I walked into my dad's office and told him I couldn't do it. I couldn't marry this guy. I didn't want to spend the rest of my life with someone who would treat me this way, even if I had a wedding dress hanging in my closet, a church booked, and a caterer reserved. I could no longer picture myself with this man forever, though I was scared to death about telling him. My life was drastically changing, and—since we weren't married *yet*—it wasn't fair for him to be pulled along on this roller coaster. He didn't feel convicted about the sex. *Only I did.* He didn't have the life-altering experience at the Passion Conference. *Only I did.* He didn't read his Bible and long to discover more and more about Jesus. *Only I did.* We were all of a sudden walking on two different roads. Our tracks were never going to merge.

I cried and cried and cried in my dad's office, and then I drove myself to my office, where I was working, and asked my fiancé to meet me there. To this day, this conversation will go down as one of the hardest conversations of my life, right up there with telling my parents that I was pregnant. Because the truth is, I did love this man. *Of course* I did—I was this close to committing my life to him, for better or worse, in sickness and in health.

I said a lot of words that morning to him. We both cried a lot of tears. I handed him the ring back that I'd been wearing as a promise to him. And then he asked me one final question. He asked me what I wanted. If it wasn't him, then what was it?

And I kid you not, I said to him these exact words: "I'm not sure what I want, but I think I want someone like that Aaron Ivey guy at church."

The man I rode in the car with to Passion. The man I frolicked in the snow with in Colorado. When God starts chasing you, He changes what you want.

And in following Him, you find Him giving you what He knows you need.

Chapter 5

It's Complicated

So, what do you think of Jesus girl Jamie?

That's what an old friend of mine actually called me during that season of my life. "Jesus girl." Felt a little odd to me, but Jesus girl Jamie was sure doing things a lot better than college girl Jamie. In fact, after everything that had happened, I decided I wasn't even going back to school in the fall, that I would work for a year before going back to college. Honestly, I didn't know if I could handle going back into the same environment where I had lived so irresponsibly. I needed a fresh start.

That's how I became working girl Jamie.

And between Jesus girl Jamie and working girl Jamie, I was happier with my new titles than all the old titles I'd ever worn in my life. I was undeniably different now—still trying to figure out how to live this Christian life, of course, and still stumbling along at it, but able to see that I was making progress. Even the trauma of breaking off my engagement had become a huge feat for me, a sign that my walk with Jesus was growing deeper. I wasn't drinking anymore, wasn't having sex anymore, wasn't even thinking about dating anymore, and my ex-fiancé and I could go back to just being friends again, like before.

Uh, Jamie, you sure that's a good idea?

Boy, do I wish someone had come along and asked me a question like that. How I wish a caring friend had stepped in and said, "Jamie, not trying to run your life or anything, because you are a 'working girl' and all, but . . . I think you're about to make a really stupid mistake." Maybe someone did tell me that, and I just don't remember it.

All I do remember is that sometime in the fall, I was asked to go on a little business trip for the company I was working for—a weekend conference up in Dallas, which super excited me, because in my mind a work trip was just the coolest thing ever. Everyone else I knew was studying for exams, going to classes, partying at night, doing all their college-student things. And here I was, heading out on the road for an all-expenses-paid business trip. Pretty grown-up, huh?

Where the stupid part comes in is that, for whatever ludicrous, ridiculous, dumb, careless, (add your own favorite idiotic adjective here) reason, I decided that asking my ex-fiancé to come along for the ride sounded like the thing to do, so that I wouldn't just be a young woman out driving alone on the highway.

Bear with me now, although I'm sure you can see where this story is going. I'd booked us at the same hotel, but in separate rooms because, first of all, I was living with different standards now and was trying so hard not to be a girl who sleeps with men she's not married to—and because, second of all, he was my ex-fiancé, and our relationship wasn't like that anymore. We were just friends now.

Still, we only used one of those rooms that weekend.

If you've ever failed in the same exact way as always, falling to a sin that you truly thought you'd put behind you for good, you can relate to how devastated I felt as a result. Even this many years later, as I'm typing up the story, the sadness just floods over me. I remember how intensely I was trying to be different. I remember declaring that I wanted to start over with that part of my life. I remember committing again that I would keep my body pure from now on, and how seriously I felt about this new promise, knowing it was what God said was best for me. I was so eager to be good. I was so much happier living the life of a Christian girl. For the first time in my life, I was trying to do the right things, not to check off a box, but because I truly wanted to obey God. And now . . .

Pull out all the pins I thought I had packed up.

Pin that letter on me again. The one I've worn before.

"F"—you're a *failure*.

The guilt that I'd felt, leading up to what became my broken engagement, had obviously been serious enough to drive me toward a significant change of life plans. Kept me from getting married that summer. Truly led me toward pursuing purity in my relationship, whereas I never had before in my life. In many ways, though, I'd never felt the kind of guilt I was feeling now. Over the next few weeks, I continually beat myself up for what I'd done. But I hope you hear what I'm about to say, because it is the gospel, through and through. God met me in the intensity of my guilt with the even greater intensity and reality of His forgiveness. Yes, I had failed. No doubt about that. And I knew I'd be living with certain consequences of my decision. But I confessed my sin to God—even this sin, this sexual sin, which had become for me the hardest thing to let go of when I started following Jesus—and I felt the most complete forgiveness of my sins that I'd ever experienced. My guilt led to repentance, not shame.

That's how, unlike all the failures of my past, God transformed this failure into one of my most significant milestones. Because even with the changes I'd made in my life up to that point, lingering doubts had kept me worrying that I was still putting on an act. Different scene, same old show. But I'd never reacted to my sin with this level of both horror and humility. If I was still the same old Jamie that I'd always been, I knew this response wouldn't be happening.

The months of wondering if I was truly in this thing for the long haul were wiped away for me in the crucible of my guilt and God's forgiveness. His gospel proved His love to me, and I knew I would follow Him forever. In my failure and in His continued pursuit and love for me, I knew He was worth it.

And I've never doubted it since.

Among the changes and fresh motivations that God inspired in me, in the aftermath of this weekend collapse, was a craving for His Word. In particular, I clung to every story in the Bible that told about someone who loved God but messed up big-time.

The truth is, of course, people messing up is pretty much the whole story of the Bible. Everybody in there was a sinful person, like we're all sinful people, and except for Jesus (because He had no sin and IS GOD), there's not a single one of them whose sin doesn't show up somewhere. But I was hunting for the *big* sinners. Like me. (I realize all our sins are big to God, that there's no such thing as a little sin. But I was in the middle of trying to rid myself of what, to me, was my own personal "big sin," and I wanted to see how somebody, anybody, in Scripture had dealt with making the big-sin choices I had made.)

I found him in David.

I was already familiar with his story, of course, as I'm sure you probably are too. But in the midst of my particular season of failing, David's story became water for my soul. The Bible calls him "a man after [God's] own heart" (1 Sam. 13:14), who God chose to be king of Israel. He was flawed but amazing, and God would use him for so many great things. He wrote many of the psalms we still read in the Bible, and his love for the Lord was absolutely contagious.

But despite his deep love for God, he made a horrible decision one night. He put himself in a position where the possibility of being lured into sexual temptation could easily happen, and he invited another man's wife to his room in the palace.

David's life, going forward, would continually bear some of the scars that resulted from this one night of sin and the other compromises that followed. I'm not trying in any way to minimize the evil of sin and how it hurts, wounds, and impacts everybody and everything in its path. But when brought face-to-face with his failures, David continued crying out to God. Most important, he never stopped loving Him. And as someone dealing with David's kind of shame and embarrassment over my latest mess-up, the experience of reading again what David did and what God did was healing to my broken heart.

I remember taking his words from Psalm 51 and turning them into my own prayer:

> Have mercy on me, O God, according to your steadfast love; according to your abundant mercy blot out my transgressions. Wash me thoroughly from my iniquity, and cleanse me from my sin! (Ps. 51:1–2)

I began to pray the same things to God that David expressed here, asking Him to cleanse me from my sin and to have mercy on me because of His enormous love for me. And God was doing that in my world. He was using my transgressions against Him to teach me His unwavering love toward me—just like He did with David after the same sort of sin.

David's failures, like I said, did bring consequences on his life. Bathsheba, the woman he slept with, became pregnant with his child. David, afraid and wanting to save his own reputation, called her husband back from war in hopes that everyone would assume Bathsheba was simply a normal, pregnant wife. But when that plan didn't work, David ordered the man moved to the front lines of battle so that he would be killed. Then David brought Bathsheba over to be his own wife, again trying to give off the impression (as if people didn't know how to count) that the baby she was carrying was legitimately theirs by marriage.

What a mess, right? David was scrambling to keep the consequences of his sin private, like a lot of us tend to do when we're afraid of being found out. And, hey, of all the telltale signs that something's not right in a person's life, a pregnant belly is one of the, uh . . . the biggest.

Ask me how I know this.

Because, yes, I was pregnant.

Again.

What in the world was going on here? How could God let this happen to me, now that I was truly following Him? It didn't seem fair, what this particular mistake was about to cost me. The freedom I'd been feeling, the forgiveness I'd been trusting and walking in—what did all of that mean? How would anyone believe I was any different now? If so, then why had I fallen back into the same struggle I'd vowed to put behind me, months earlier?

I don't quite know how to describe the embarrassment I was feeling. Not only did I wonder if others would doubt my faith, I began to wonder myself if my faith would sustain this trial. Even though I believed I'd really changed, was it still just me trying hard to be good, or was I genuinely trying to follow Jesus? Those are two distinct things, of course, and they came together to form the two questions that dominated my mind after my positive pregnancy test.

Where was my life headed from here?

And what was I going to tell people?

The first people I told were my parents (again), and although I'm sure they were thinking, *What is wrong with you, Jamie?* they at least didn't act that way. Maybe they also saw something in me, something different than before. The first time I'd gotten pregnant, I really felt the type of worldly guilt I described earlier. Embarrassed maybe, or even humiliated over the consequences that my sexual sin would bring me. I hadn't meant to get pregnant, obviously, but that was just the risk everybody was running. And in my mind, pretty much everybody was out there running it. That's why I had such little regard for committing myself to marriage, with little if any repentance for the lifestyle I'd engrossed myself in.

This time, though, I was broken. And I think they knew it and saw it in me. I was *so* sorry for my actions—a sorrow that I'd already poured out to God, before it spilled out here in front of my parents. This time around, I was scared for what people would think about me, because I was different now. I truly was. And I was worried my failure would taint their trust in me, because I wanted my outsides to mirror the change that God had worked on my insides.

So it was the same . . . only different. Much different. And that's what we as women need to remind ourselves—that we can respond to our sins and failures *differently* than we used to do. Trust me, I know about feeling as though I should always have my stuff together and never fail. But failing is what we do best. All of us. We're all human; we all sin. Yet we can respond to it differently—with deep repentance, but not despair. With a guilt that leads to repentance.

And while I do still wish someone might have noticed and caught me before I set off toward a tragic weekend (we need those people in our lives), I am forever grateful for the support system (specifically my parents) who loved me through this ordeal. Part of being different—both in our ongoing lifestyle, as well as in our comebacks from sin—is the result of people who are closely around us and keep pointing us back to Jesus. We must serve that role for others, and we must seek others to play that role for us.

Whatever you're going through today—maybe something not too unlike the story I'm sharing, or maybe something else that's been equally troubling to you—don't do it alone. Don't try it without people supporting you, telling you the truths of God's Word, and constantly pointing you to Jesus.

I see it all the time in the women I meet at the jail. I constantly hear them share about their support system—the people around them who remind them of the truth, who hold their hand when they're struggling, who believe in them and love them no matter what. The girls who are most likely to succeed when they're released are the ones who have a support system in place. Many of them, like I was, are struggling so hard to let go of things that have a real hold on them. For some, it's drugs; for others, sex; for others, money. Either way, when they make the same mistakes over and over again, they need someone there to love them, accept them, and point them to Jesus.

That's what my parents were to me at that time. I'm sure they were upset with me for my choices. I'm sure they wondered if this might just send me sprawling back to my old ways again. Yet they didn't seem ashamed of me. They continued to care for me, support me, and keep Jesus squarely in my headlights. And as I look back now on this part of my life, I'm still in awe of the way they loved me through it.

Unlike the last time, I certainly didn't entertain the thought of marrying my baby's father. I'd already decided he wasn't the man I wanted to spend my life with. I knew he wasn't committed to following Jesus, and I wasn't going to let a baby alter my decision to wait for a man who *was*.

So, with the advice and support of my parents, we decided to tell very few people about my pregnancy, for which I was grateful. I did tell a few friends, as well as a pastor and his wife at our church, and also my aunt and uncle who lived in California and were aware of the change in my life over the past few months. It was our little secret, which we all knew eventually would be something we'd be forced to tell everyone. (Hello, baby in my belly!) But every day meant trying to figure out what life was going to look like at our house when this baby arrived. And just like last time, I began to fall in love with my baby.

I was at work one day, several weeks after finding out I was pregnant, when I began to feel some extreme pain in my lower abdomen. Over the next few hours the pain increased so much that I decided to drive myself to the hospital. (Dumb idea, I know, but I was twenty-one and clearly had a reputation of making dumb decisions!) I called my dad from the car, telling him my plan, when the pain became so intense that I had to pull over and wait for him to come pick me up. He arrived quickly, and together we drove on to the hospital—my dad there, like always, to help his baby girl.

So here we go—worried again that something was wrong with another pregnancy. It had only been a year and a half since I'd previously walked down this road. And whether you're married or not, the thought of losing your baby is tragic. I didn't want to go through that kind of sorrow a second time. I was scared.

And wouldn't you know it, but someone else from our church was seated in the emergency room waiting area when we arrived. You should have seen my dad trying to explain to this man, without spilling our secret, why his daughter was here, all while being deeply concerned and trying to comfort me. I was hurting too bad to really help much, but he was somehow able to fumble some words together, enough to apparently satisfy this person's curiosity.

Then finally—if you've ever been an emergency room patient, you know what I mean by *finally!*—they called my name and escorted me back to a room, where doctors and nurses tried to figure out what was causing me such extreme pain, which was increasing drastically. Before long, it was clear the baby was in trouble. And maybe me too. Something had ruptured, calling for immediate surgery because I was losing blood so rapidly.

From there, things were mostly a blur. I remember my mom being with me outside the operating room. I remember people moving really quickly around me. I wasn't in extreme pain anymore, but was loopy from all the meds I'd been given. I signed the necessary papers about the possibility of losing ovaries and what not, and then I was out, while they opened me up.

I awoke to the good news that I hadn't lost my ovaries, but to the bad news that I had, indeed, lost my baby. I had an ectopic pregnancy (an ectopic pregnancy occurs when a fertilized egg implants somewhere other than the main cavity of the uterus), and the embryo had implanted inside my ovary, and then had burst—apparently quite uncommon. My surgeon, an older man, said I was only the second patient he'd ever seen in his entire career with this kind of condition.

So that morning I'd been pregnant, and by that afternoon I wasn't. It had happened again. I'd lost another baby.

And still today when I think about this memory, I cry. So much shame, intermingled with so much sorrow. All these feelings were battling with my heart because I didn't want anyone to know I was pregnant for fear of what they'd think of me, yet I desperately wanted to mother my baby. It was a war I wasn't prepared for, a battle I didn't know how to fight.

And at the end, the only prize left to me was another letter to pin on my chest.

Another "F"—*fraud.*

I felt as though I was a fraud of a woman. Two babies lost, at twenty-one years old, and I couldn't tell anyone about them. To the handful of pastors from our church who came by to visit me and the few others who knew I was in the hospital, we told that I'd had a cyst that ruptured. A plausible story, close to the truth, but certainly not the whole truth. The pregnancy remained our little secret, a secret that would continue to haunt me for years to come.

Oh, if only I'd known then what I know now. All the stuff that was still ahead of me at that moment—the war I would continue to fight internally—could largely have been avoided. My love for the babies I had lost, my failure to even grieve their deaths well because of my fear of being found out, my suffocating shame at not being good enough—I kept it all inside. I tried toughing it out all alone. How I wish I could've just said, "Look, everybody, I made a really poor choice, and because of that, I got pregnant. And I am so sorry, more than you know. But I still love Jesus, I'm not through following Him, and I am truly a different person because of Him. I am only here because of God's grace and forgiveness, and I want to live to worship Him every day for it, for what He's still going to do in my life to change me."

That's what I wish I would've said. Or something like it. But I didn't. I didn't say it because I didn't think they would've believed it, and some days I struggled to believe it as well.

But I'm here today to tell you—nothing good comes from not being known. I say all the time now that my journey toward following Jesus was super messy. I stumbled my way toward trusting Him. I fell flat on my face more times than I can count, and this story of my pregnancy is only one of those ways. I see women all the time who doubt their commitment toward God because of their messiness. They begin to follow Jesus, they give Him their lives, then they make a poor choice—usually a choice they've struggled with for years—and they feel as though they can't do this Christian life. *I get it. I've been there.* Those feelings are real. But they're also not truth. I know you may really feel like a failure, but it doesn't mean you *are* a failure. I know you really do feel unforgiveable, but you're not!

After my pregnancy, I had so many doubts about my ability to follow Jesus. I was so mad at myself for this mistake, and wondered if I would *ever* be able to be a woman who didn't do what I kept doing. A lot of days I didn't know because I'd proven myself such a failure. My failures, not God's forgiveness, were what kept and controlled my attention. I was dwelling on all that I had done wrong, instead of dwelling on all that God had done for me. My sin ruled my thoughts instead of the glorious grace of Jesus.

But I also began to understand how deep the love of the Father is for His children. My big sin (once again, all sins are big, this one just seemed super-duper big at the time) that I thought was so awful had already been paid for. God knew all the days of my life before I was even born, and He still chose to love me and pursue me. This is true for those of you who are stumbling your way toward Jesus as well. God knew how you would turn your back on Him, and He still chose to love you. God knew how you would harm your marriage, perhaps even destroy it, with one poor choice, and He still chose to love you. God knew you would struggle to accept your body so much that it would lead you to purge food from your system daily, and He still chose to love you. God knew you would drink so heavily that you would make choices that hurt those around you, and He still chose to love you. God knew you would have that abortion, and He still chose to love you.

God *loves* you.

His love is unending and cannot be thwarted by our poor decisions in life. His love is bigger than our capacity to even understand. His love is something we can hold on to when the rest of our world seems to be crashing down.

If I told you I believed these things to be true in the weeks and months following my failure and its aftermath, I'd be lying to you. Believing these truths about God took me years to grasp. For years, the secrets of my pregnancies haunted me and I feared being found out. I thought if anyone knew I'd gotten pregnant while I was following Jesus, they would declare me a fraud. Somehow I had elevated this one sin to the highest level, and I was certain everyone around me had elevated it to the same extent.

But struggling doesn't make you a fraud or a failure. Struggling through your faith is not an indication of lack of faith; struggling through your faith is an indication that you are fighting for your faith.

My prayer for you and for me is that we would be women who acknowledge we're struggling and that we love God with everything we've got. Those two can exist together: struggle and loving devotion. You're not a bad Christian because you're struggling with something. God is not ashamed of you, and you shouldn't be ashamed of yourself either.

I remember talking with my friend Maria about this part of my past. She had been struggling with infertility, and I decided to share with her about my miscarriages in hopes that somehow my pain would help her know she wasn't alone.

It was one of the first times I'd been able to open up about it. At this time in my life, I was still so hesitant about sharing my stories for fear of what someone would think of me . . . And if I was too out-front in talking about how I was trying to follow Jesus, and then I messed up big-time again . . . what would people think?

All these fears. All these worries.

Oh, what they do to us, when God just wants us free. Free to struggle without fear. Free to love Him without risk of tarnishing His faithfulness.

For as we talked that day, Maria didn't once make me feel less-than. You'd be amazed, once you dare to try it, how often you'll get this kind of response, not the one you dreaded and dreamed up into a monster. She just listened to my stories as I shared about the darkness God had brought me from. I'd said it, and it hadn't killed me. In fact, it made me feel God's love for me.

The next time I saw Maria, she said she'd brought me a little gift. (I have friends in my life who are the best at giving spontaneous gifts for no reason, and it always makes me feel so loved. Don't you just love gifts for no reason? Let's all go do that today! Buy someone a gift for no reason and see how it makes that person feel!)

She handed me this little bitty box, and when I opened it, I found a necklace inside, with two angel charms hanging from it. The meaning didn't strike me at first, and maybe she saw the confusion in my face. She smiled and told me the charms represented my two babies that I had lost to miscarriage all those years ago.

Oh, my, the emotions that rolled over me at that moment. Maria had not only listened to my story without judging me for my past, but had stepped into my journey by presenting me with this gift. She'd acknowledged the pain I had been through, and reminded me that God was in control of even the hardest parts of my story. What's more, my telling it had connected with a tender part of her own story—her infertility—and had given her a way of turning her struggle into something beautiful and caring, a painful place she could use to bless others rather than being consumed inside her own anguish.

Those charms became a longtime reminder to me that the parts of my story I felt were so hard to share were actually the tools God had given me to help unlock others' suffering and share the healing only He can bring to all our broken places. They didn't make me a failure. They didn't make me a fraud. They just made me a woman completely dependent on the love and grace of her heavenly Father.

They're all part of what it means to follow Him.

Chapter 6

Come, Thou Fount

In my mind, a pastor and a girl like me didn't exactly make couple material. It was one thing to say I wanted to date someone like that Aaron Ivey guy at church. But to actually do it? To actually have that kind of relationship? To have that kind of boyfriend? A good one? I don't know.

I mean, yeah, I was following God now, loving Him the best I knew how. He was truly moving mountains in my heart and life. I had come to know Him in ways I'd never experienced before. My whole sense of "normal" had begun to change. But still, this didn't change the fact that I had failed Him *bad*. And being able to date a good guy so soon after my last ginormous failure would be a little too much to ask, now, wouldn't it? That's what I was thinking. *How much good stuff do I need to do before I can expect, or even accept, this kind of blessing?* (Is that anti-gospel or what?!)

But as God would have it, just a few months after my second pregnancy and miscarriage, that super-nice Aaron guy from church *did* ask me out on a date. Remember, he had asked me out a year earlier, but . . . I knew better then, and I'd turned him down. He may have thought I was what he wanted, but—if he only knew, huh?—he didn't really want to attach himself that closely to somebody like me.

This time, though, when he asked, I said yes.

But in saying yes, I wasn't only saying yes to a date. I was saying yes to a whole lot more. There's no way a guy like him and a girl like me could just casually go out for a few months and then move on. It was either going to work forever or not at all. The only way I could agree for him to see me, I knew, was if I let him really *see me.* The real me. With all my dirty laundry to air. Then after he'd seen it, I assumed he'd do one of two things: he'd either run away as fast as he could, or he'd run to me and stay by my side forever. And if I had to guess which one he'd pick, I was pretty confident he'd be out. Either way, it would be up to him. He deserved to know what he was getting into.

So that's what I did. Or at least that's what I told him I was *going* to do. On our first date, I said I had a "few things" I needed to share with him. When I was ready. Which I wasn't, quite yet. But when I was, I'd tell him. I would. I promise.

I felt in that moment as though I were Cinderella on a first date with the prince. On the outside, here was this beautiful woman in her fairy godmother gown who looked like she deserved to be keeping company with such a great guy; but on the inside, she was terrified he would find out her true identity. She knew she was as much princess material as I am *American Idol* material. Tone-deaf people like me don't become superstar musical artists. And girls like Cinderella who've spent most of their lives covered in dirt—they don't get the prince.

So, on one hand, Cinderella was *this* close to being able to enjoy the freedom of loving someone, and of being loved herself. She was *this* close to feeling totally comfortable in her own skin, confident, completely at peace, made new all over again. All except for one thing—this one *huge* thing—that was hanging there in the way.

Her identity was holding her hostage.

And I just couldn't let that keep happening to me anymore. What I'd done had done enough. I couldn't stand letting it keep doing it to me for the rest of my life.

So I told Aaron I'd let him know when I was ready to fill him in on all my junk and, to my disbelief, he just said . . . "Okay."

That was it.

Okay.

He didn't ask a single question about it. The conversation just moved on. Like nothing had happened.

Okay.

All right, then, so here we see one of the eight million ways that Aaron and I are different. If that had been me, I would at least have asked for some sort of hint. I mean, is what you need to tell me something about jail time? Drug use? Do you have an STD? Are you missing a pinky toe? Come on, give me *something.* Put me in the ballpark. Don't leave me dangling to fill in the tantalizing blanks with whatever my wild imagination could think to scribble there.

And yet he didn't ask me even one more question on the subject. Nothing.

I guess you wouldn't be surprised to know, then, that the longer we dated, the more I knew I was falling in love with this man—this man who (side note here) had never kissed a girl in his life. And now here he was with *me,* the girl from church who (true story) everyone said he shouldn't be hanging around with, the one whose "few things" she needed to share with him involved, among other things, a lot of past sexual sin. Oh, and two unplanned pregnancies. No biggie.

What had I done to deserve someone like this? Better question—what all had I done to *never* deserve someone like this? In my entire dating life, I had never felt with anyone what I felt with him. I almost had to teach myself how to date all over again, since I'd never dated anyone as a woman who was following Jesus.

In my previous life, we would have had sex on our first date. Or even before.

In my previous life, I would have based our relationship mostly on our physical chemistry.

In my previous life, I would have felt loved because of what we did when the sparks started flying.

But this was so different. At times I felt lost. I wondered how he felt about me. I wondered if his love was true. I wondered how to love him well. I wondered a lot of things. I'd just never been in a relationship with a guy where I was loved for me instead of for what I could do for him. It was wonderful and terrifying all at once. On one hand, I desperately wanted things to be different so I would know I was truly changed. I loved waking up each day to see where our relationship was going next. But on the other hand, I often wished for the old ways because . . . well, at least I knew how to handle those situations. Dating one of the church pastors was obviously not that kind of situation.

Like, when you're dating a youth pastor, one of the things you find yourself doing is volunteering in the student ministry. So I was sort of in leadership now—sort of—since I was the girlfriend of one of the real leaders. Because wouldn't that make logical sense? To most people? But the truth is, even though I was twenty-two, I remember sitting through the worship and the teachings as if I were one of the kids in the youth group. Technically I was one of the "leaders," even though I was in the same boat spiritually as the students I was helping to lead. Because even though I'd practically grown up in church, all I'd really picked up during those years was a bunch of head knowledge. Experiencing real intimacy with God was all new to me.

I felt so inadequate. So out of my element. This dating a pastor was making me do things and feel things I'd never done or felt before.

I'd have to say this is where my journey of shame truly began. Or at least where it truly intensified. I was trying to live up to a title. Because, after all, if I was the youth pastor's girlfriend, I should have it together, right? What if all these people I was hanging around so closely now—the high school girls, the other leaders, even the main pastors of the church—what if they knew what my life truly looked like seven years ago? Even *one* year ago?

So I began to stuff all the feelings and memories of my past deeper inside, hoping that if I said the right things and did the right things, I would surely look like a "good" youth pastor's girlfriend. That way, maybe no one would ever ask me about my life before I met Jesus or the road I'd walked when I was younger. It would be my little secret between me and God. He had forgiven me, the Bible said, so now I just needed to act like a good Christian girl.

Block all the rest of it out.

But that wasn't going to do. I'd already told Aaron I would tell him. And pretty soon, I couldn't hold it in any longer.

At the end of May, we were on a trip with some of our students on South Padre Island, a resort town on the Gulf Coast, down at the southernmost tip of Texas. All spring I'd been asking God to confirm in me the moment when I should share my story with this man I was coming to love so dearly. I'd prayed for God to soften Aaron's heart, to make him ready to hear what I knew would probably land on him with a shock, even though I guessed he'd probably been bracing himself for the worst. I could only imagine how someone who'd saved himself sexually for marriage would feel hurt and uncertain when he realized the one he loved had not.

I was so afraid of what would happen when I was completely honest with him. I was broken over the "me" that I was giving him. He was a man of God with a great future ahead of him. And to be honest, he might have just been better off with someone a bit more put together than me. Someone more holy. I had been following Jesus for a little over a year, not to mention I'd been pregnant nine months earlier. In my mind, Aaron was getting the short end of the stick in this relationship, and I wondered if he would think the same thing after I opened up to him. If he decided he didn't want to be with me anymore at that point, it would've made all the sense in the world.

But as I was about to find out, love oftentimes doesn't make sense. Not when God is involved.

What happened that night on the beach is one of the most special moments of my life. Rarely if ever have I so tangibly felt the love of the Father. We'd shared a supersweet time of worship on the beach with the students, we'd all taken Communion together, and then everyone had dispersed to their rooms. I stayed on the beach, undetected by everyone leaving. In my heart, I knew it was time. Tonight was the night I would lay it all out on the table. God made clear He was with me. It was time to let Aaron into my whole story.

I have no idea how long I sat there in the sand alone before he eventually came out looking for me. At the time, I was lost in praying, crying, begging God to make this easy. For me. For Aaron. Only in looking back does it make me giggle that God would choose a moment when we were out of town for me to do this. I mean, if things had gone bad, it would have made for an awkward bus ride back home.

But Aaron found me in the same spot where I'd been all night. He sat down in front of me, his back to the ocean. I think he knew, too—this was it. This was the moment when I would tell him all those things I couldn't say five months earlier. I was finally ready.

Even as I type these words, I can still hear the waves crashing against the sand, like a metronome of my heart. One beat after another, one crash after another. The moon was our only light, as though we were alone on an island and the rest of the world had disappeared. The glow of God's presence seemed to be all around us as we entered into one of the most intimate spaces we'd ever shared together. As the story poured out of me.

And I held nothing back.

I started from the beginning, just as I've done with you in this book, and all the shame and all the sorrow came bubbling over through tears that streamed down my face. I don't remember how long I talked, but I do remember that Aaron never wavered—never looked surprised, was never annoyed, never upset. Nothing but love shone through his eyes. The whole time. Till I'd said everything I'd been wanting to say.

There. I'd done it. I had said it. All.

And what would happen next, I honestly didn't know. Would our relationship continue? Maybe so, maybe not. I had been feeling as though it was about to go somewhere, somewhere really special, but it was all hanging on this moment. Would I prove to be simply too much for him to handle? I would have been devastated if that were the case, but I had come to terms with the fact that he might just walk away. And I'd decided I could live with that—because in opening up my heart and telling all the truth about myself to Aaron, I was doing more than just letting the man I loved into my mess; I was also trusting God with this story for the first time as well. Trusting Him enough to share my mess with someone I loved. And even if my ugly story wasn't going to end up being safe in Aaron's hands, I knew it was safe in God's hands. I knew He would do something special with this moment, even if it didn't lead to anything special anymore between Aaron and me.

In my sixteen years of marriage, I can only think of about five times when I've seen Aaron cry. But that night, as I was talking to him, as we held hands on the beach and looked into each other's eyes, tears began falling down his cheeks. I could tell they weren't tears of anger, disgust, or regret. He was crying real tears of sorrow. Crying *with* me. Compassion and love were overflowing as he rubbed my hands while I shared. The only time he let go of them was to wipe away tears from both of our cheeks.

After I finished, I stared at him through the tears in my own eyes and waited for the results. In my deepest of hearts, I wanted him to stay. But in my flesh, I knew he didn't have to. No one would have blamed him if he'd bailed and decided this was just too much. People had already advised him to steer clear of girls like me, so it would've been no big deal for him to raise the white flag and leave the relationship.

But instead, his words to me set the precedent for my healing from shame that would continue over the next ten years. Because even though it would be a long time before I could share these parts of my story with anyone else, I knew in that moment this man would be by my side until one of us left this earth.

He looked at me and said, "You have nothing to be ashamed of or embarrassed of, Jamie, because that's not even the girl I know. You aren't defined by your past. I love you."

It was—and still is—the most Christ-like encounter I've ever experienced with another person in my entire life. It gave me a glimpse of what it felt like to be seen the way God truly sees me. I knew in my head that God delighted in me, that He loved me, that He cared for me, that He believed in me, that He forgave me, that He could (and would) use me for whatever good purpose He desired, that I was still capable of bringing Him glory. But my heart would often try to convince my head that those things weren't true. Yet He used this indescribable moment with my future husband to proclaim to me through a human voice all the things about my true identity that He was already declaring. He used Aaron to be an example of the love of Christ for me.

I was changed forever that night.

By telling it all. And by receiving even more.

And for that reason, I've never felt another day of shame in front of Aaron about my past. Not once. We don't even need to talk about it anymore. It's not part of our normal day-to-day conversations. I just know. That night on the beach proved his love and acceptance of me. All of me. The good and the bad. It was done. And it was incredible—as anyone who's ever felt the relief of getting their secrets out in the open will tell you.

I had known Jesus loved me and redeemed me, and I didn't need Aaron to accept me to make any of that any more true. It sure did feel good, however, knowing I was loved by my Father in heaven in spite of myself, and also by the man I would eventually marry.

Yet even as loved and accepted as I felt in that moment, I continued to live in fear of what others would think of me and how I would be perceived. So in many ways—in most ways—I kept hiding the pain in my heart, along with the true experience of my redemption. It would still be many more years before I'd finally learn this important lesson: When we hide the mess we've been through, we also hide the redemption that God has lavishly poured on us.

We can't proclaim His grace until we expose our mess.

Every Tuesday, as I've mentioned, I get the joy of spending two hours at the local jail with women who want to learn about Jesus, helping them figure out how to do life again once they are released. It's a seven-week program. We talk with them about creating a résumé, dressing for a job interview, finding safe housing, getting a bus pass, finding a rehab center—all the things they need for re-entry into the world.

But we also talk with them about Jesus in one way or another. Some weeks we share Him through our prayers and conversations. Other weeks it's through presenting the gospel to them in a way that hopefully makes sense. Because more than anything, we pray their lives will be changed. More than we want them to get good jobs, we want them to know how much they are loved, adored, cared for, and treasured by the Creator of the universe. We want them to know that their true freedom comes from Jesus.

One week after class, a few of us were chatting, and Sara (one of the women we'd met there) was sharing with us her plans for the next few years. After her release, she hoped to get into a certain program that would help her get back on her feet. She desperately wanted this to work, and I sensed she was actually hopeful for her future. She had been in jail before, been in rehab before, even been in the program before that she was now so eager to get into again.

But beyond hoping she was finally on the right track this time, she was wrestling with a much deeper question as well. Would God, when He looked at her—when she was on the outside— would He still see her crimes? Would He still expect her to pay time for her sins, the way she was doing now in jail?

Makes sense, doesn't it, why she would ask that. Why wouldn't the same principle that held her in jail translate into her future? Why wouldn't she need to keep paying for her sins until a holy God decided she'd paid enough?

She was certainly right about one thing. Our sins *do* need to be paid for. But not by us, we told her. That was done by Jesus on the cross. We need to believe in what He's done and stop trying to do the impossible ourselves. Because when we are followers of Jesus, the only thing God sees when He looks at us is the righteousness of Christ, not the guilt of our sins.

For a split second, I saw something in her eyes I hadn't seen before. A sigh of relief went almost visibly through her body. You could tell the gospel had clicked with her.

Freedom. Forgiveness. No more guilt and shame.

And even as we were explaining this to Sara, her reaction reminded me how I'd felt, too, in my early years of following Jesus. I'd known I was covered in His righteousness. I'd known I didn't deserve it and couldn't do anything to earn it. I'd known salvation was a free gift from God. But sometimes I wondered if I could be good enough to take away all the bad things I had done in my life.

Truly, Sara is just like us. As a follower of Jesus, she is free. Clean and forgiven. Righteous before God. When He looks at her, He doesn't see her past; He sees only the girl He loves because of what Jesus did over two thousand years ago.

It would be years before I truly understood this.

Thirteen months after that conversation on the beach, Aaron and I would be married. Throughout our dating and engagement, we had grown in our love, and I had grown in my relationship with the Lord. Yet as much as I felt loved by Aaron, in the back of my mind I always felt so used and dirty. I just couldn't seem to let it go. I knew God had redeemed my life, but it didn't change the fact that I had been sexually active since I was *sixteen* years old. Neither God nor Aaron ever did anything to make me feel condemnation, but I so desperately wished I could change my past.

As our wedding day approached, I started to become anxious about the intimate aspects in our marriage and what it would be like when we started sharing those together. I worried that I would know too much, or would seem too comfortable with it that first night. I desperately wanted our wedding night to feel new and different and special. While all my friends who *hadn't* had sex were praying for things to go well on their wedding night, praying for it not to hurt too much, I was praying in the *other* direction. I was asking God to strip away any memory of sex, to make me *uncomfortable*, in fact, in the intimacy of the first night. I wanted Him to literally make me feel as though this was the first time I had ever done it.

I had shared some of these concerns with my friend Rachel. And the night before our wedding, she gave me one of the sweetest gifts ever—a letter that spoke so deeply to my heart. I still have it to this day. I cherish her words to me so much. And while I know this letter is a little long I promise it's worth it, and I have a feeling you might really need to hear it all, the way I needed to hear it that night.

It went like this. After apologizing for not having enough money to buy me anything else—*Ha! We were college students then!*—Rachel wrote:

> God gave me something very precious that I believe He wants me to give to you for your wedding gift. The other day I was just flipping through my Bible and these words jumped off the page. God spoke volumes to me as I read this passage in Ezekiel. As I thought and prayed about

what I could give you as a gift, God spoke to my heart
and told me to give you these words from HIS love letter.
I pray that God speaks directly to your heart words of
hope, peace, and love. You are awesome, and He wrote
these words for you . . .

She then wrote out the entire passage from Ezekiel 16:8–14,
which I'm going to print out for you, too, because whatever God
says in the Bible is a whole lot more important than anything else
I've been trying to write here.

Ezekiel 16 is a prophetic description of how God treated His
people after many generations of their idolatry and rebellion, enough
that He'd been forced to discipline them severely by allowing the
Babylonians to invade and conquer their land, hauling them off into
captivity. So in these verses, He speaks to them as though they'd
been an adulterous woman, yet He does it in language that could
only come from a Husband who wanted nothing other than to see
them clean and pure and restored to wholeness again.

Here you go, then . . .

Later I passed by, and when I looked at you and saw that
you were old enough for love, I spread the corner of my
garment over you and covered your naked body. I gave
you my solemn oath and entered into covenant with you,
declares the Sovereign LORD, and you became mine.

I bathed you with water and washed the blood from you and put ointments on you. I clothed you with an embroidered dress and put leather sandals on you. I dressed you in fine linen and covered you with costly garments. I adorned you with jewelry: I put bracelets on your arms and a necklace around your neck, and I put a ring on your nose, earrings on your ears and a beautiful crown on your head. So you were adorned with gold and silver; your clothes were of fine linen and costly fabric and embroidered cloth. Your food was fine flour, honey and olive oil. You became very beautiful and rose to be a queen. And your fame spread among the nations on account of your beauty, because the splendor I had given you made your beauty perfect, declares the Sovereign LORD. (Ezek. 16:8–14 NIV)

I'm getting chills at this point, as I was reading. I had been praying such crazy prayers, I thought, realizing there was *no* way God could truly answer them in the way I was hoping He would. And yet right here in the Bible was my Father in heaven, talking to someone just like me, telling me exactly what He plans to do with His children who've made such a mess of their lives that they can't clean themselves up any other way, unless He does it for them— something He not only *can* do, but actually *wants* to do because He loves us so much.

Rachel finished her letter like this . . .

I know that God has made you a new creation—it is so evident. God has restored you from the pain and regrets of your past. You are completely pure in the sight of the God who has created you. He has washed you, adorned you, and put a crown on your head and called you beautiful. Isn't that so incredible? Isn't HE so incredible? We serve such a faithful God, who takes so much delight in the work of restoration.

Tomorrow as you dress in your wedding garments, remember how Christ dressed you. The reward He has given you is priceless—an incredible, godly man who loves Christ and you. I pray that your love for each other grows over the years. You and Aaron have been such a testimony to Matt and I. I am so honored that you would let me be such a special part of your wedding. I praise God for you and for our friendship. You are so awesome, and I love you so much. I pray that tomorrow is the most wonderful day of your life and the beginning of a thousand more! Thank you for everything! Happy Wedding! Have sweet dreams! —*Rachel*

Whew! Huh?

Rachel got me. She knew me. She understood how desperately I wanted to be a new creation sexually. But what she was trying to remind me—what I had forgotten—was that God had already done it, more completely than I could ever ask or dream. He had made my whole person a new creation by doing something only He could do, something He does because of the gospel. As the Bible says, "If anyone is in Christ, he is a new creation. The old has passed away; behold, the new has come" (2 Cor. 5:17). Because of Jesus, and only because of Jesus, I was able to hold my head high as I put on my white wedding dress to marry the man of my dreams.

Aaron, of course, never knew me during my wild and crazy days. He only knew what I had told him. (Which, I'm sure you believe me by now, is more than enough!) But I knew the great work God had done in my heart, as did a handful of people in the church on that day. My parents, for instance, had walked through so much with me, and they stood there to testify to the truth of how He'd made a new creation of my life. My best friend, Amy, who knew all the stories from my past, stood beside me as I proclaimed my love for Aaron and how far God had brought me in my walk with Him.

That's why, although every bride is able to remember the details and moods and feelings of her wedding day, I had something a little extra to celebrate as the doors of the church opened and the bagpipes began to play "Come, Thou Fount," a song that meant so much to me then, and even more to me now.

My dad and I looked down the aisle to my waiting groom, while everyone stood. I felt so proud of the woman I had become. I could feel my dad beaming with pride, too, for what God had done in both of our lives. Although not everyone in the room knew where I'd been, they all knew where I was going and that Jesus had changed my life.

As I walked toward my future husband, I sang the song in my heart that, to this day, I can hardly sing without my eyes welling up with tears.

> Come, Thou fount of every blessing
> Tune my heart to sing Thy grace;
> Streams of mercy, never ceasing,
> Call for songs of loudest praise.
>
> Teach me some melodious sonnet,
> Sung by flaming tongues above.
> Praise the Mount! I'm fixed upon it,
> Mount of Thy redeeming love.[2]

Do you know it? Can you hear it? You want to just sing along with me? Come on . . .

Here I raise my Ebenezer;
Hither by Thy help I come.
And I hope, by Thy good pleasure,
Safely to arrive at home.[3]

This is the part of the song—this next part—where, every time I sing it, the tears begin flowing. For although I grew up in the church, I was truly a stranger to God until He sought me out. I knew a lot *about* Him, but I had been so far *from* Him. Still, He brought these incredible words to life—in *my* life—just as I hope He's done in yours.

Jesus sought me when a stranger,
Wandering from the fold of God.
He, to rescue me from danger,
Interposed His precious blood.[4]

And then that last verse. Oh, that last verse . . .

O, to grace how great a debtor
Daily I'm constrained to be.
Let Thy goodness, like a fetter,
Bind my wandering heart to Thee.

Prone to wander, Lord, I feel it,
Prone to leave the God I love;

Here's my heart, Lord, take and seal it,
Seal it for Thy courts above.[5]

I can't think of a more perfect love song I could have sung to my heavenly Father as I made the walk down the aisle to my husband. We had chosen this song because we knew how God had rescued both of us from danger by sending His Son for us. We knew we were prone to wander, and we were begging Him to seal our hearts, both to Himself and to one another. We were committing our lives to Him as the Savior of our souls and the author of our salvation, wanting to love Him and love each other well for the rest of our days.

With the possible exception of that night on the beach with Aaron, never before had God's kindness been more personal to me than when I stood with my groom in that church. When God changed my life and I started following Jesus, I never imagined He would lavish such love on me by giving me a man who not only loved me dearly, but who also saw Jesus in me and not my past.

I was finally learning to receive God's loving-kindness.

If I'd only known how sweet it could be.

But you know what? I still didn't realize even then—even standing next to Aaron, even with my redemption on such dazzling display in that life-defining moment—just what Christ had died to do for me, how complete and utterly boundless His grace is for me. It would be years before I dealt fully with the shame that entangled my heart, while I continued to believe if I could just act the part, I could overcome all the bad stuff by doing all the good stuff.

What I quickly learned, however, was that acting the part is suffocating to the soul. There's only one way to end the bondage and finally settle into freedom. Would I have the courage to open myself even wider than I'd already done, so that I could be more contented and confident in Him than I'd ever been?

Chapter 7

Owning My New Identity

Remember at the end of high school when they announce the people who are "Most Likely to _____"? Then they fill in the blanks with things like, "Most Likely to Succeed," "Most Likely to Stay Single," "Most Likely to Become Famous." You get the point here.

I never received any of those "Most Likely to . . ." awards in high school, but I can only imagine what I would have received if they'd given me one. As I told you before, my identity in high school was squeaky clean. Sure, I did things I shouldn't have done, but nothing worse than any of my other friends were doing. It wasn't like I was leading the tribe in sneaking out and getting drunk; I was just one of the many people doing it. The nice, church-girl, overachiever image was enough to counterbalance everything.

So my "Most Likely" would have consisted of super normal things: "Most Likely to Get Married Early," "Most Likely to Become a Teacher," "Most Likely to Become a Mom." Yet on the inside my identity was in shambles. I knew I wasn't "likely" to do any of those things. And as I worked my way through college, the predictions would only have gotten worse: "Most Likely to Get Divorced," "Most Likely to Get a Disease," "Most Likely to Get Pregnant." (Well, that one actually did happen, but thankfully not the others.)

If we're not careful, our whole identity can become wrapped up in what other people think we're supposed to be or what we think we're supposed to do. Perhaps today, for example, you're basing your identity on something as fresh and recent as how you acted last night and what somebody said to you or accused you of. Or you're finding your identity in the mom you want to be, or the mom you hate that you are. Maybe you're finding your identity in the job you have, or the job you wish you had but can't seem to get hired for.

Maybe you find part of your identity in what you did this summer, or what you wish you'd done this summer, compared to what everybody else was doing (and bragging about doing). Maybe you find your identity in the ministries you perform at church and how people perceive your "Christian" standing because of it. Maybe you find your identity in your passions, in your body mass index, in your checkbook balance, in your home décor choices, or whatever other kinds of indicators seem to measure your worth and success as a person. We are constantly finding our identity from everything around us, from everywhere we go, and from everything people say and think about who we are or who we should be.

But this is not who we *are*. And we always need to remember that.

A few years ago, one of my kids came home from school, super down about his day. He just wasn't his chipper self when I picked him up. And when we arrived home, he went straight to his room and wanted to be alone. I feel this way myself sometimes, so I gave him his space. But when I circled back around to see him later that night, he started to unfold the story for me.

He told me how during the day, some kids at school had been talking about all those "Most Likely to . . ." categories, and his friends announced they had voted him "Most Likely to Lose at Arm Wrestling." My first inclination was to laugh. From my vantage point as an adult, of course, being known as the best arm wrestler in third grade doesn't mean much. But I held back my giggles because I could see this insult had been a real blow to my son's nine-year-old heart, because his friends had made him sad . . . and "because I'm strong," he told me.

"I know you are," I said, pulling my sweet boy close to me, hugging him. Now, I didn't do the "my kid's better than your kid" thing by telling him he was stronger than everybody else. I also didn't tell him his friends were stupid and that I'd beat them all up if he wanted me to. (Although I did think that!) I just whispered into his ear, telling him he was a child of God whose identity was already secured, and that his identity in Christ is the only identity he ever needs to be worried about. He didn't need to be devastated or heartbroken over what his friends were saying, because that identity never matters.

And I wonder if that's not what our Father wants to do when we come home from another day of combat, with all those false identities screaming in our head. Can't you just hear Him coming close and saying, "My sweet daughter, those thoughts you're thinking are not true. Remember My promises to you? My Word is true. You know this. You are a child of Mine. You are a new creation. I have made you alive with Christ, and I have chosen you to be My daughter so that I can do great things through you."

Over and over I've needed Him to whisper these truths to me—through His Word, through His Spirit, through my community. And if past (and current) history are any indication, I feel pretty sure I'll be struggling to believe it until the day I take my final breath on this earth, until I'm face-to-face with Jesus. Of the numerous things in my life that I battle nearly every single day, *remembering my identity* is one of them. It's been that way from an early age, as I imagine it's probably been for you.

When Aaron and I got married, I was still a complete mess about my identity. All those memories of guilt, all those memories of my shortcomings, all those memories of my sin—they all came back to haunt me. Even with my whole future ahead of me, even with everything God had done to chase me down and rescue me from the path I'd been following for so long, my past was still what I thought defined me. Therefore, despite my husband's love for me, I couldn't seem to shake those thoughts of being defiled, unlovable, unclean, and disgusting. At my lowest points, I even wondered if Aaron ever thought those words about me.

And goodness sakes, this whole "pastor's wife" title, while a wonderful thing to be—well, you can imagine why this was problematic for me. How in the world could *I* be married to a pastor? I was constantly wondering what people would think of me if they truly knew what I'd been through the past few years. Would people be asking if someone like me could actually serve God? Would they trust me as a true Christian? I mean, do "real" Christians get pregnant by someone who's not even their boyfriend when they're supposedly committed to following Jesus?

For some reason, I felt as though being a pastor's wife came with certain iron-clad requirements. It wasn't just *given* to you; you had to *earn* it. Only the best Christian women in the church could marry a pastor, and I didn't feel anywhere close to that. I was still under the skewed impression that being a leader meant you were better than others, that if you really loved God, you never messed up. And I'd messed up a lot. In fact, Satan, and the lies of my heart, had spent many years convincing me that I was worse than anyone else, that my failures were so grand that people would never be able to see past them.

So how had I ever ended up in this "pastor's wife" camp? I felt so inadequate for it.

But let me just clear the air really quick for all of you who may be wondering. Pastor's wives are real people. They lose their temper just like you do. They go to the bathroom just like you do. They cry in movies just like you do. They get jealous just like you do. They get promotions just like you do. They've probably even let a curse word slip out of their mouth a time or two, just like . . . well, maybe that's not like you, but then again, maybe it is. Pastor's wives are normal people, just like you. And if you're in a church that creates a culture of putting its leaders on a pedestal, where they're better than the rest of the church, I ask you to question how it's affecting people who walk into your church feeling broken, in need of love and acceptance, and already not feeling good enough to receive it. For while God's Word does say that leaders and teachers are held to a higher standard, I'm also a firm believer that leaders of churches should be vulnerable with their people.

No one should be left wondering if those in positions of spiritual authority are above having any struggles. If the leaders of your church have never admitted to sin struggles from their platforms, you might need to find some new leaders. I despise the day that I ever quit admitting my own need for a Savior. My wretched heart is still so prone to wonder.

Okay, getting off soap box now. Let's carry on.

I knew in my head that I was forgiven, that Jesus had taken on my sin, and that I was a new creation. But I struggled so much to truly believe it. I carried so much shame around for the first few years of our marriage, shame that took years for me to untangle. I told you earlier about the "pins" I felt destined to wear, and that if anyone knew of them all, I would surely be discredited. So I was determined to be such a good person that no one would suspect all these badges I continued to pin on my chest. If only I was good enough, I thought, no one would know—which, for me, meant respecting my husband as humbly as I could, going to as many Bible studies as possible, working on all the teams I served on, not drinking alcohol or doing any of the other crazy things I'd done in my past. All I needed to do was keep being good, keep trying to get everyone else to have a good opinion of me. I was always fishing for a better identity than the one I carried around in my heart and mind, based on how well I was performing as pastor's wife Jamie—trying so hard to be good, while constantly thinking that people thought the worst of me.

But over time, God began to reveal Himself to me in ways I'd never been willing to accept. He allowed me to believe things about myself that I had not been believing before. I finally started to learn that my identity is not skewed because of all the things I've done or haven't done, but is secured by all the things Jesus has done (as well as by what He hasn't done, like condemn and reject me). My identity is only what it is today—a daughter of the King—because of Jesus. It has nothing to do with me.

So I'm not "most likely to" anything anymore, in terms of who I am in Christ. "Most likely" has been replaced by *absolute assurance* that I am loved and cherished by my heavenly Father, despite all that He knows of me. And when I finally began believing this truth—that God could use a broken, messed-up person like me (yes, even a broken, messed-up pastor's wife) for His glory—I could finally breathe a sigh of relief. That's when things really started to change for me.

I know it can be the same for you.

You are a chosen race, a royal priesthood, a holy nation, a people for his own possession, that you may proclaim the excellencies of him who called you out of darkness into his marvelous light. Once you were not a people, but now you are God's people; once you had not received mercy, but now you have received mercy. (1 Pet. 2:9–10)

God's Word says some amazing things about us—that we are chosen, loved, equipped, made worthy. Once we were a bunch of nobodies, but now we are children of God. Not just children of God, but a "royal priesthood."

This is one of my all-time favorite elements of our identity. Priests were essential throughout the Old Testament in helping people experience their relationship with Almighty God. The priests came from a certain family line, having been chosen from among the entire nation for this special office, able to petition and offer sacrifices for the atonement of the people's sins. Nobody else could do this. Being holy and set apart was part of their identity. And today, because of what Christ, our great High Priest, has done for us in the sacrifice of Himself, everyone who's a child of

God is now a full-fledged member of His "royal priesthood"—not because of anything we've earned or accomplished, but simply because that's who God declares us to be.

And notice this. Among the reasons for why He's set us up as royal priests is so we can "proclaim [His] excellencies." Now, if this new identity we held was based on our own efforts, if it wasn't based solely on the broad shoulders "of him who called [us] out of darkness into his marvelous light," the main way we would show His greatness would be through doing good things, from doing all the right things. And while His beauty does come shining through us when we trust and obey Him, we actually proclaim His excellencies the loudest when we tell people how we used to be in darkness, how He brought us into the light, and how He continues to love and pursue us even when we fail.

I didn't get that for years. I thought I was still building my identity. I thought I was still overcoming my past, constantly playing catch-up in order to compensate for it, always needing to prove—to God, to others, and even to myself—that I was good enough to belong, especially with all my baggage. But when we are finding our identity in anything other than Jesus Christ, we are setting ourselves up for failure every single time. We are leading ourselves down the old, familiar pathway of . . .

Shame.

Ugh. Let's talk about shame. Mind if we talk about shame?

I'm guessing you don't mind if we do, because shame is where so many of us have walked (and continue to walk). Perhaps you're one, in fact, who's kind of given up hope of ever being able to walk anywhere else than in shame, without its clouds and shadows hanging over you.

I'm afraid I'm way more familiar with shame than I'd like to be. According to *Webster*'s dictionary, *shame* is "a painful emotion caused by consciousness of guilt, shortcoming, or impropriety." Shame is what hits us when we remember things we didn't do well, places where we fell short of measuring up. The memory of it—the "consciousness of guilt"—is what brings shame on. And let me tell you, if you don't already know it yourself from firsthand experience, it is suffocating.

If the Enemy had his way, *shame* is what we'd all take on as our identity. All the things we think about ourselves, all the things we've done, all the things we haven't done, all the things we worry that others are seeing and concluding about us—all of it would become blended together into what we'd naturally define as our identity.

But let me shoot a little straight with you here, because I think this is something we all need to hear, myself included. As believers and followers of God, here's our identity: We are women who are being cleansed, changed, and "conformed to the image of his Son" (Rom. 8:29), so that we look more like Him every day. We are daughters of the living God, covered in Christ's righteousness, set apart for His own wise and merciful purposes. "Even as he chose us in him before the foundation of the world, that we should be holy and blameless before him" (Eph. 1:4). *This is our identity.* And what prideful people we are whenever we put our own shameful thoughts about ourselves above the thoughts that our loving heavenly Father has said He thinks about us.

The death of shame in our lives is tied to believing that *His* view of us is greater than the *world's* view of us, and especially greater than our *own* view of ourselves and of our sin. We must stop creating our own identity based on our past or other people's perceptions, and start walking out the identity that Christ has given us. You are not defined by your marital status, your mothering status, your online status, or any other status, but only by your eternally secure status as a CHILD OF GOD.

Edward Welch, author of *Shame Interrupted*, says, "To be human is to experience shame, but to be human is also to hope. The ashamed person doesn't want to remain unclean forever, and he or she doesn't have to."[6]

Because Jesus has given us a whole new identity.

Each week at the jail with the women we serve there, our time begins with someone sharing from God's Word. Our love for them is so deep that we crave for them to trust Him with their lives. Whether while gathered there in the room with us or in the stillness of their bunk after hours, we pray they'll decide to follow Him with all their hearts. It's our biggest desire for them.

Recently we were circled up in the group discussing boundaries, and—as is almost always the case, no matter what we're talking about—the subject drifted to these girls' aspirations of being loved and wanted. It's amazing to watch these needs surface during every single conversation we share with them. To say I don't understand why this happens would be a lie. Don't we all understand this deep desire of theirs?

So, as we were supposed to be discussing healthy boundaries, a woman named Rachel began describing all the ways she was identified by the people around her, using words not suitable for this book or probably any other piece of adult material. As I listened, my heart broke for her and continued to break further with every word she uttered.

Rachel had lived the life of a prostitute for many years, and—well, let me just say, I know how easy it can be to stereotype someone who's resorted to this lifestyle, but I refuse for you to judge her, because you don't know her world. Neither do I, but I've learned a lot about it from my time spent with these women in the jail. We can't judge someone for the shoes they walk in, when we've never had to put those shoes on our own feet. We just can't.

Anyway, tears began to slowly fill her eyes, soon spilling over and rushing down her cheeks as she talked. She felt so worthless. She believed every single identifying word she'd been told by those around her, all the verbal pins she'd laid out there for the rest of us to see.

I'll be honest, I have no idea if Rachel is a follower of Jesus. I know she heard about Him for the weeks she was in our class, and I continue to pray she is letting Him reach her in the deep places of her heart. But in that emotional moment, I connected eyes with Rachel, as tears began trickling down my own cheeks as well. And I spoke truth to her. People had ascribed a lot of "Most Likely" badges to her future, and I wanted her to know those shameful predictions were not hers to carry around for the rest of her life.

I told her that no matter what she thought of herself, and no matter what anyone else said about her, she was not any of those things. They didn't define her. I told her that God loved her no matter what she had done. I told her that these things from her past were not her identity, whether she lived the rest of her days behind bars or whether she created a new life for herself outside those walls. I told her that Jesus said, "I am the light of the world. Whoever follows me will not walk in darkness, but will have the light of life" (John 8:12), that He can change her identity, same as He'd changed ours, and could call her His own.

There's only one reason why I was able to proclaim the excellencies of Christ in that dark place of haunting memories and crippling shame: because I knew from personal experience where He'd brought me from, to place me in His marvelous light. These weren't just spiritual ideas I was sharing with her about her identity; they were truths I'd seen take root in my life, tugging up big, ugly clumps of fear and shame that had buried their claws in my heart for as long as I could remember.

My story, like your story, is not the story that others have written about us, nor is it the thick autobiography we've felt the need to write about ourselves. Our stories are redemption stories—the stories of redeemed identities. We were lost, but now we are found. We were orphaned, but now we are adopted. We were unloved, but now we are loved. Unacceptable, now unconditionally accepted. Disgraceful, but now showered in grace. And when we operate from that true identity in Christ, who knows how many Rachels could catch their first glimpse of something greater about themselves than the story they've felt doomed to live out.

Your identity is not a bunch of wishful thinking, pasted into the Bible in hopes of making you feel better. It is the solid ground of who you really are, now that Jesus has shined His forgiving light on your situation. Cling to it. Believe it. Claim it as your own.

You and I don't have to walk in shame or in others' shadows anymore.

All our "Most Likely" losses have been redeemed by the Most High.

Chapter 8

Sin Shock

I t's so hard to be like Jesus," my friend Andrea told me one Sunday at church. We were sitting on the front row (because I'm a good pastor's wife, and that's where I sit—obviously!) chatting about some hard things from her previous week. She was clearly frustrated with certain people, and their sins, and their actions, because each of these sins and actions were affecting her and her family. She laid it all out there, lamenting how hard it can be to treat people the way Jesus did. I nodded along, but I haven't gotten that phrase out of my head.

"It's so hard to be like Jesus."

Isn't that the truth? It's so hard to be like Jesus, and yet the Scripture says to "be imitators of God, as beloved children. And walk in love, as Christ loved us and gave himself up for us, a fragrant offering and sacrifice to God" (Eph. 5:1–2). So being like

Jesus is what we're explicitly told to do, and yet it's so challenging to actually do this—to walk with the love that Jesus showed, to give ourselves up for people the way Jesus did.

Jesus encountered people all of the time who were struggling with sin, and in all His encounters with them, He was never once shocked by their sin. He was disheartened by their sin; He was broken for their sin; He would eventually be condemned for their sin. But what we never see Jesus say to someone is this:

> "How could you?"
>
> "I'm so ashamed of you."
>
> "Who do you think you are?"

No, and the reason we don't see Jesus react this way is because He knows something about people. We are sinful people. "For all have sinned and fall short of the glory of God" (Rom. 3:23). Every single one of us. Jesus never encountered anyone who hadn't sinned, and yet He loved them in the midst of their sin. This is why it's hard to be like Jesus. He loved no matter what. He continued to pursue. No matter what. He stepped into messy situations. No matter what.

Now, before you get upset with me, let me clarify something again, in case you were sort of skimming over the last couple of paragraphs. Yes, Jesus is offended by sin, because all sin is against Him. Yes, Jesus is appalled at sin, because all sin is against Him.

Yes, Jesus is outraged over sin, because all sin is against Him. But in all my years of reading about Jesus, I've yet to find a time when He is shocked by sin. Taken aback by sin. Flabbergasted by sin. There's no "Really? Again?" or "You seriously need to get your act together."

Never.

But can I just go out on a limb here, and say that we struggle to be like Jesus? Being like Jesus is hard on many levels, of course. (Understatement of the year, I know!) But this "not being shocked by sin" is one area we really struggle with. We are often shocked at people's sin when it's revealed to us or when they confess it to us. We think . . .

> "I would never do that!"

> "I thought you were better than that!"

I call this SIN SHOCK. And it's a problem in our lives and in our churches. I believe it's one of the major hindrances to women becoming free from their guilt and shame. You won't find this term in the dictionary, although after a quick Internet search, I did find a Japanese movie called *Sin, Shock* (weird, right?!). Still, I'd like to think I made it up. Even if I didn't, it's my book and I can say whatever I want. Moving on.

Sin shock occurs when someone confesses their sin, or their sin is brought to the light, and people around them are shocked by what they're seeing and hearing. I get it. We all do this, sometimes without even knowing it. We take on the posture of someone who could never do such a thing as the person who's confessing to us has done. We push people away with our words and/or body language. Whether we intend to or not, we create a space where confession is not wanted or welcomed. But I want us to think about what this does to the culture we're trying to develop in our churches and other relationships.

I have a dear friend who's struggled with worry and anxiety throughout much of her life, which have led to many crippling bouts with depression. Sometimes the weight of it has confined her to bed for days, fighting stomach pains and so much more that's been brought on by this condition. I'll never forget one day when we were talking about this, and I asked if she'd ever talked to anyone at her church about her struggles . . . because maybe if her community knew about it, I figured, they could help walk beside her through this battle.

What she said next has never left my brain, and it's the essence of what sin shock does to a community. She told me she wasn't ready to tell anyone about it because her husband was going through the process of becoming a deacon, and she wasn't sure how they would feel about her (and him) if they knew about her struggles. The reason she hadn't told anyone was because of what they would think of her, because of what she either rightly or wrongly perceived as their potential sin shock.

I have cried so many tears over this epidemic in our church culture. I have cried tears over my own struggle with this. I have cried tears over women choking down their battles with sin, living all alone with them, out of fear for what the rest of us would think. Let me tell you right now . . .

This MUST change.

We need to be creating a culture in our churches where people feel the freedom to confess their sins BECAUSE WE HAVE JESUS. We need to be creating a culture where people are expected to come regularly to each other in repentance BECAUSE WE HAVE JESUS. We need to be creating a culture where people can talk about their struggles BECAUSE WE HAVE JESUS.

God's Word is clear that "none is righteous, no, not one" (Rom. 3:10). Paul himself confessed, "For I know that nothing good dwells in me, that is, in my flesh. For I have the desire to do what is right, but not the ability to carry it out. For I do not do the good I want, but the evil I do not want is what I keep on doing" (Rom. 7:18–19). And yet, in almost the next breath, he tells us, "There is now no condemnation for those in Christ Jesus" (Rom. 8:1).

What if we truly just admitted that we all sin, we all mess up, we all let others down, and we'll all keep on doing it until the day we die. Why? Because we are sinners. We are human. We are fallen people in desperate need of a Savior. It's who we are.

And what if we truly believed that those around us will let us down, goof up, make bad choices, and struggle through life until the day they die too, because they're all sinners, same as us. They are human. They are fallen people in desperate need of a Savior. It's who they are.

If we are to imitate Jesus, one thing we must begin to do is allow people to confess and repent in a safe place, because Jesus constantly provided a safe place for sinners to be transformed. We must be churches, and groups, and friends, and women who say to one another that we value confession and repentance over secrets and perceived perfection, because there's no need for pretending to be people we're not.

John 8 tells about an encounter between Jesus and a sinful woman, where He saves her life both physically and spiritually. This story is one of my favorites in the Bible, because I can relate to this woman on so many levels. I have felt what she must have been feeling in that moment. And if you've never read this story for yourself, or if you haven't in a while, I encourage you to drag out your Bible, dust it off, and prepare to fall in love with Jesus again in the eighth chapter of John.

Jesus was teaching people early in the morning at the temple, when the scribes and Pharisees (enforcers of the religious law, basically) busted up His teaching and demanded something of Him. They were trying their best to catch Him doing something wrong so that they could convict Him of a crime, expose Him as a lawbreaker of the Old Testament so they could convince everyone He wasn't who He said He was.

These men presented Jesus with a test case—a woman who'd been caught in the act of adultery, having sex with a man who was not her husband—and made her "stand in the center," humiliated, embarrassed, ashamed, mortified, disgraced—all the feelings of someone whose junk is thrust out into the open for everyone to see.

"In the law, Moses commanded us to stone such women," the men said to Jesus. "So what do you say?" The Bible just comes out and reveals their motivation: "This they said to test him, that they might have some charge to bring against him" (John 8:5–6).

But you know what? Jesus flipped their whole worlds upside down. (This is one of the many reasons I love Jesus so much.) He was so calm. He never looked at this woman in disgust. He never wondered how she could possibly do such a thing. He never condemned her, not once. He simply said to the people demanding justice at her expense that, yes, justice could be done . . . but only if they, too, had no sin within themselves. "Let him who is without sin among you be the first to throw a stone at her" (John 8:7).

This only left one person capable of starting the rock throwing that would punish this woman with death for her sin. The sinless Jesus had every right to stone her. Every right. Yet He knew something this woman didn't know, and that the Pharisees didn't know—the fact that her sin would be paid for, but not on this day. And not by this woman. It would be paid in God's good time by Jesus Himself.

So don't think for a minute, with Jesus knowing what human sin would ultimately cost Him, that He didn't view sin as ugly and awful and horrific. He hated it then, and He hates it now. But shocked by it? Did Jesus appear shocked by her sin? No, after all the other men had walked away, when it was just Jesus and this woman . . .

Okay, can you even imagine what this must have been like? Let's try for a second. Put yourself in her position. You've just been caught in the worst sin you can imagine committing. What sin would that be for you? Maybe you've already committed it, and no one knows about it. It's your little secret. Covering this sin has become your main agenda each day. You work on keeping it hidden all the time, creating ever more elaborate disguises to shield it from public view. But now your ugly sin—this ugly sin—is out in the open, and people are demanding your life in payment for what you've done. Imagine that you are alone, vulnerable, exposed, humiliated, standing in front of the Savior of the world. Standing before your Jesus. Totally ratted out.

Now. Expecting to see some holy shock?

"Jesus stood up" (because He'd been stooped down writing stuff on the dusty ground with His finger), "and said to her, 'Woman, where are they? Has no one condemned you?'"—to which she said, "No one, Lord" (John 8:10–11). What's going to happen next? The gravity of her situation rests in His hands.

But, oh, my sweet Jesus. I love Him so much. He showed so much love, grace, and freedom to this woman. He didn't negate her sin; in fact, He told her, "Neither do I condemn you;" . . . but not before saying to her, "Go, and from now on sin no more" (John 8:11). He did not condemn her for her sin. He would be condemned for her sin. Justice would indeed be done for her sin, but not at the hands of her accusers. Jesus Himself would justify it. Our Savior. Our Redeemer.

And this is how we're to treat our friends, our sisters in Christ. We can't condemn them because we, too, are like the Pharisees. We are full of sin ourselves. But we can love them well, we can bring truth to their lives, we can show them the words of God, and we can point them to Jesus. We can hate their sin, we can encourage confession and repentance, and then we can step into the battle with them.

My friend who struggles with depression—who was worried that if she confessed it to people in her church, they'd think less of her and look down on her husband—is a picture of what should never happen in the church of Jesus Christ. And yet, don't we know, it happens ALL THE TIME. Most of the women seated around you on Sundays, most likely including the woman who's sitting there looking lovely and smiling to people across the room, are afraid that if others knew their struggles, they'd be disqualified from doing the work of God.

But if I was sitting across the table from you right now, I would hold your hands, look into your eyes, and beg you to be a person who never makes another woman feel that way. Be a person your friends know is safe. Be a person who values people and their lives and their journeys. Be a person who, when presented with sin, takes people to the Redeemer who died for that sin and who's even now in the business of redeeming us all from our sin. Be a friend who points people to Jesus for confession and forgiveness.

I admit, in the past, I was shocked by people's sins every single time. I would hear a story about a person failing miserably who claimed to love God, and I was unbelievably shocked at how they could possibly have done something like that. But the longer I live and the more often I see people failing, the more I realize I'm one step away from failure as well. One step away.

That's why this fight is more important to me now than ever. It's not that I've grown cynical and hardened to human failing. I've just seen too many women hurting, and seen what Jesus can do when we actually begin to imitate His heart. My own sin will always look better or worse depending on the day, but some things must always be kept unchanged in our eyes: the holiness of God and the depravity of man. These are unchangeable realities, yet by God's grace and by the blood of Jesus, they can become the ingredients for total freedom without condemnation.

All of us are the woman caught in sin.

And all of us want to be treated the way Jesus treated her.

I remember when I first shared online the story of my pregnancies from college. My first pregnancy was difficult (because no one signs up to be a teenage mom), but my second was even more difficult because no one wants to be a follower of Jesus whose sin is so out there in the open for everyone to see. I was doing my best to follow Him when I got pregnant that second time, but my flesh won the battle. My heart knew what was right, but my flesh wanted its own way. I knew I had changed, that I indeed loved Jesus dearly, that I truly desired to do the things He had asked me to do. But then all of a sudden, I'd messed up again. My sin struggle was back. I was looking for love and acceptance in the same place I'd been doing it for so many years. And what I'd found again was guilt, shame, fear, and a desperation to keep my sin unknown.

Almost no time after I'd posted this story, women began emailing me left and right, telling me their own stories too—their sin struggles, their shame, their silent secrets. Time and again in what they wrote to me, I began noticing this same phrase appearing somewhere in almost each message: "And no one knows." All these stories—laced with so much shame, guilt, pain, sorrow, anguish, poor choices, consequences, all of it—and yet each seemed to carry a consistent thread. These women had been carrying that story around for years, all alone.

No one knows. Certain sins come with their own calling card, one that advertises what we're struggling with, no way to hide it. But in most cases, women walk around with struggles that no one can see, and that they're too afraid to tell us about. One of the people who contacted me was a woman from my own church who told me she'd had an abortion in college, and no one knew. She was married now, a momma to three, and still holding on to a buried memory that no one knew about. In spite of her knowing she was forgiven, she was living with a secret that caused her to feel unknown by her friends and family. Meanwhile, Satan continued to bring it back up, causing her to feel shame and guilt over and over again, while all along Jesus was there with her, forgiving her, offering her complete freedom from this pain.

But where were the other women in her life? Where were the people in her church and community who could hear her story, learn of her past, and not register such shock at what she was saying? Did she not know any women like that?

I guess I've learned from being around the ladies at the jail for so many years that there's not much that can shock me anymore. Prostitution, drug rings, sex trafficking, alleged murder. Maybe part of our problem is that we've kept ourselves too sheltered within our own little cosmetic worlds, where tragedy is not being able to find a close parking place when it's raining, or running low on hand sanitizer during flu season. But when we make it hard for people to confess their sins and ask for help—whether believers (who we shouldn't expect to be any more perfect than we are) or unbelievers (who we shouldn't expect to act like Christ-followers anyway)—we are setting them up for disaster. We are creating a culture that says to people, "It's better for you to lug this guilt and shame around with you than to confess it, bring it out into the light, and let Jesus deal with it. Maybe it's better that we never know."

And I say that's what should shock us.

One of the subsets of sin shock that's probably worth addressing on its own is when the sin in question is not just that of a friend or acquaintance or maybe someone we don't even personally know, but rather is a sin that involves you or impacts you directly. The times when it's hardest for us not to be shocked by someone's sin is when the fallout is going to be played out right in front of our face. Am I right?

Imagine with me the wife who's hearing her husband confess his pornography addiction for the umpteenth time. She will struggle with not being shocked by this sin, since it's affecting and hurting her at such close range, creating tremors throughout her marriage, her whole identity, her entire life.

Then there's the daughter who hears that her father has left her mom for another woman. This girl will struggle to not be shocked by her daddy's sin, more than the friends and neighbors who hear about it later, because it affects her and hurts her so dearly.

Then there's the student who hears a teacher she greatly admires admit to a failing that removes him from the classroom. Or the congregation that witnesses the confession of their pastor, setting up months and years of unnecessary upheaval and turnover. These confessions hurt to hear—more than most—because they affect us where we live. They're much more difficult to process.

Several years ago, someone very close to me opened up about their infidelity. This wasn't just a random person, but someone I love dearly. And when the phone call came, I broke. I reacted out of disbelief. In fact, my exact words went something like: "How could you do this to your family? How could you do this to all of us? You know how bad this hurts, because your dad did the same thing to you. Don't you remember the pain you went through?"

See, when it's something up close, when the proximity to our heart is so point-blank, it's hard to view sin the way God views sin. We are humans. With emotions. We hurt. We get mad. Then sad. And there's nothing unusual about this. I'm not out of reality enough to suggest that you could just stoically stand there and not be crushed by what you're hearing and discovering. There's not much of a way around that.

In fact, sin is worth being angry about. Sin should disgust us, should repulse us, should bring up emotions in us that produce anger. Anger toward sin is righteous. God is repulsed by our sin every single day—angry at where it comes from, angry at what it does to us, angry at its offense to His absolute holiness. But God is never repulsed by us or overwhelmed at how to do anything about it.

So while I compassionately understand how certain sins, in certain situations, committed by certain people in certain levels of intimate relationship with us can incite an unsurprising rush of outrage, grief, and apoplectic shock, the truth remains (and God, in His grace, can bring us to see this) it is still a sin that Jesus died for. And if we persist in being shocked by it, all our "How could you?" and "I would never" statements will only succeed at building thicker, higher walls between ourselves and those we love, and will make the other person's ability to seek and receive God's forgiveness that much more slow and painful. For all of us.

Ugh, it hurts all over again when I think back to that phone call where I went so ballistic in response to that person's sin. We recently had a conversation, and for the eight millionth time I apologized for my reaction. They've totally forgiven me. We actually moved forward pretty quickly after that initial phone call. I've repented of my anger toward them, and have continued to love them and walk with them through their journey. But I'm still reminded of it often, the shock and devastation I displayed in that moment, wishing I had responded differently. Sin shock is in many ways no less damaging than the offending sin itself.

Who am I to think I have the right to hold that stone in my hand, ready to throw it, even when the target is no more than two feet away from my breaking heart? I still must drop my stone and admit I'm the same as them. Desperately in need of Jesus.

My friend wasn't lying when she said, "It's so hard to be like Jesus." Everything about being like Jesus is difficult. But there's hope. We don't have to do this alone. I always say there are three things that will get me to the end of my life loving Jesus.

God's Word + The Holy Spirit + Community = that's how I'll make it.

The great thing about God's Word is how it truly lights our path. It provides the hope we so desire as we journey through life. When Jesus was preparing to die, He comforted His disciples (and us, as we read His words) by telling them He would be sending them a Helper.

> "These things I have spoken to you while I am still with you. But the Helper, the Holy Spirit, whom the Father will send in my name, he will teach you all things and bring to your remembrance all that I have said to you." (John 14:25–26)

This "Helper," the Holy Spirit that God sent to us, is here to help us remember all that Jesus has said and done, to keep His Word speaking to us, reminding us of the truth it teaches. So while being like Jesus is hard, the Holy Spirit is inside to help us, even to help us do hard things.

When we allow ourselves to be a safe place for women to confess their struggles, we are imitating Jesus. And when we find ourselves struggling to be that place for women, we have the Holy Spirit inside us to remind us of all the things Jesus taught us. He reminds us how Jesus treated every sinner He came into contact with, all who realized they were sinners. He loved them,

He forgave them, and He commanded them not to sin anymore. God's Word and His Spirit can keep us grounded in that.

Then, community. It's a catchy word in the Christian world, but it's a vital thing that in my life will get me to the end with Jesus. Not only does God's Word remind me of all that Jesus did for me and all the ways God loves me, but my community reminds me of those things as well.

I have a group of girlfriends I like to call my "fight club." These girls know almost everything about me, and in spite of all they know about me, they continue to push me toward Jesus. They continue to listen to my struggles, and they continue to be a safe place for me to confess my sin. (Do you have a "fight club" like I do? If not, no worries, but it's time now to go and find one.) As they listen to me fight through some of the same old sins of pride, greed, power, and control, they aren't shocked by my sin, but they tell me to fight my sin. They don't think less of me as a Christ-follower, but they push me not to give in to these pleasures of the world, and to continue bringing my struggles to the light, because in the light is where freedom is found.

I've learned over the years that when we become people who encourage confession and repentance, when we make spaces for these things to happen in safe environments, freedom is the result. There is freedom in confession. There is freedom in repentance. There is freedom in knowing that your struggle, your sin, your pain, your shame, your guilt is all welcomed at the table. They are welcomed because of what Jesus, our great High Priest, did for us on the cross.

I'm declaring an end to sin shock . . . because there's no end of possibilities once we're free of it.

Chapter 9

Vulnerability Breeds Vulnerability

Pornography is a *tricky* thing that not many women want to talk about. In fact, most people assume that women don't struggle with pornography and have zero desire to look at it. I'm here to tell you differently. Those assumptions are false. Pornography may be more heavily viewed by men, but women also view pornography and are drawn into its evil traps on a daily basis. When I was growing up, pornography was something you were forced to seek out if you wanted it. You had to rent a movie, buy a magazine, or go to an establishment, but today it's very different. Today it's almost like pornography finds *us*.

The first time I remember seeing porn was when I was a child, around the third grade. We were visiting some friends of my parents, and I found a magazine in the bathroom. First of all, who keeps a *Playboy* magazine in the bathroom when you have children in your home? Whatever. I found it, I saw it, and it made me feel different on the inside. I could tell instinctively, even as a young kid, that I was looking at something I wasn't supposed to be seeing, yet I was feeling something I'd never felt before, and I didn't understand why.

The next time I remember seeing porn was during college. I was dating a guy who suggested we watch it together, and at the time I didn't see any reason for saying no. The warning flag of conscience I'd felt so strongly as a nine-year-old didn't wave so furiously at me anymore. Pretty soon, watching porn with him became normal to me. But one day, when I was over at his place and he was away at work, I found myself watching alone. And in that moment, I was struck with knowing it was wrong. I could tell it had some sort of hold on me.

Over the next few years, I didn't struggle with this desire too much, and after I started following Jesus and got married, it was basically nonexistent. I do recall one time trying to watch a scandalous movie on TV. But it was airing on one of those channels we didn't subscribe to (probably Cinemax, or as I've heard it called before, "Skin"-emax), so it was barely audible or visible through the static. I don't know why I wasted thirty minutes of my night listening to the grossness of what was happening behind all that fuzziness. But I have a feeling it's because this temptation was tapping into a desire that had been stirred up in me at a young age.

And unless I fought it—fuzzy TV or not—I would find a way to gratify it.

But there was also a more recent time—more recent than I'd like to admit—when I felt that old familiar allure again. It wasn't that I was necessarily wanting to look at porn; I just wanted the feeling that viewing it would produce in me.

All the variables were right for me to seek out some sort of comfort. Aaron was out of town, all the kids were in bed, I was teaching at church the next morning (yes, you read that right!), and my stress level was rather high. I would like to say I have no idea why I reached for my computer, but I know *exactly* why I reached for my computer. I'm a wretched sinner who, left to myself, will believe the lies of my heart—if I can just have *that*, I will finally be happy—that tell me something other than God will be more satisfying to my soul. It is so strong sometimes. And because Satan knows my past, knows my struggles, knows what will bring me down, well . . .

To search for pornography at our house, you have to know how to beat the system. You can't just type in "naked" and get what you want, because we've installed safeguards all over our computers. In fact, as I was writing this chapter, I was looking up a statistic on women and porn, and my computer basically wouldn't let me. I was restricted from that content. It was doing its job well today!

Praise God, right? We're raising children in a time of history when pornography can be accessed so easily, sometimes by complete accident. Two of our kids have accidently stumbled upon a picture on the Internet that I would describe as soft porn, and our other two kids were shown porn by another kid at the beauty salon. I was in the other room, and this still happened to my babies. I was *right there* while another kid showed them a video on his mom's phone. Porn has its way of finding you, and it always aspires to devour you—which is why we've put up these safety nets in our house—on all our computers and devices. So when I tell you I was needing to beat the system, you see what I'm talking about.

But I was lonely. And tired. And stressed and everything.

And I started searching.

But which words could I possibly type into the search engine that wouldn't be flagged and emailed to Aaron, who sees all the searches from our computers? (And don't worry, a couple of his close friends see all his searches as well.) Which words would be generic enough to sound reasonable but still take me to the websites I wanted to reach? I was basically a thesaurus that night, looking for words that were kind of bad, but not too bad.

I felt weird doing this. I knew it was so wrong. Yet something inside me craved those salacious images, more than I desired doing what was right. My flesh was determined to win this battle, and I had become its willing, though conflicted, accomplice. At one moment, I was hoping Aaron wouldn't just randomly call to see how I was doing, wouldn't prevent me from probing deeper for what I wanted, but then I was half hoping he *would* call so I'd be forced to stop, snap myself back to what I knew was right. At one moment, I was nervously hoping my kids wouldn't wake up and need me for something, but then I was half begging that one of them *would* call out and interrupt this insane searching.

I know it's gross. I'm embarrassed about it. But that's what I was doing. (Are you sin-shocked yet?) That's what the battle was like in my heart that night. Ever fought one of those battles yourself? If not to gratify your flesh with porn, with something else?

Thankfully (yippee to the safeguards!), I never found the right synonym to help me carry out my wishes. But when nothing had worked, I then began to be flooded with guilt. I mean, I hadn't technically succeeded at failing, but I'd tried really hard to do it, desperate to relieve my stress, fear, and loneliness by running back to the place I went all those years ago to manage these kinds of emotions without needing to involve God. My flesh had wanted what it wanted so badly. And I had been close to going all the way over the cliff in search of it. So very close.

I lay in bed and cried myself to sleep, overcome with guilt and shame for what had gone down during those thirty minutes. The war for my affections had been raging that night, a moment where

I realized how far I would go to meet my own needs. It was eye-opening for me and utterly terrifying at the same time.

By the next morning, I was no better. If possible, I was even *more* broken over my sin, and *so mad* at myself. How did this happen? I'm a pastor's wife. People invite me and trust me to speak to the women at their churches. I love Jesus with all of my heart. I have four kids. I'm happily married. I have a great sex life. It didn't make sense.

Except it makes perfect sense. I am a desolate sinner, in need of so much grace and mercy. I sin every single day in all kinds of ways: jealousy, pride, anger, take your pick. But this one was different for me—not the normal, everyday sin I'm used to battling. It was a ghost from my past that I thought was gone forever, and yet it had come bellowing at me the night before. I wish my ghost from the past was that I gossiped too much, or wanted money too much, but instead my ghost is sexual sin, such an intimate thing. And having been haunted by it again, my head went on a roller coaster of emotions. I felt so defeated and crushed. Because if I would do *that*, then what *else* would I do when Aaron was out of town? Did I still love God? Was I giving in to all of my earthly desires? I know it sounds drastic and a bit overkill. But when you struggle with something in your past and you give it over to God and it shows up again, you get scared. Scared of the way that this sin could grab a hold of you and take you down. If you don't get scared, then you should.

Are you with me?

Do you know what I'm talking about?

Actually, if I know anything right now, I know as you read my story, you are thinking of your own past sin struggle that sometimes creeps back into your world when you least expect it. It's that one thing you hate that you used to do or think about, and you pray to God you never have to deal with it again. It could be an affair you had, the way you lied and cheated your way to the top, the binge eating you used to do, the way you used to vomit every day to keep the figure you worked so hard for, or the words you used to tear everyone down around you. Whatever it is, I get it.

And God gets it. In fact, He talks about this exact struggle in the Bible. Paul said to one of the New Testament churches, "For the desires of the flesh are against the Spirit, and the desires of the Spirit are against the flesh, for these are opposed to each other, to keep you from doing the things you want to do" (Gal. 5:17). Our flesh and the Spirit inside of us are waging a war for our souls. Some days this war is visible to the outside world. You might choose to flirt with a man at work, knowing good and well you have a husband and three kids at home. Some days this war is over internal things that aren't as obvious to those around you, like choosing to bite your tongue when you're angry, instead of lashing out at everyone around you.

We all struggle. And we will *always* struggle for as long as we're here on the earth, even as God continually works within us to show us the incredible blessings and benefits of surrendering to Him in obedience. Because of Jesus, we can win these battles, one at a time, day after day.

But part of winning is letting others in on our struggle.

And the sooner, the better.

That's why the next morning, I found my friend Annie at church and gave her the "we need to talk right now" look. We tucked away into a classroom, and I spilled it all. It was overflowing from me, and I needed to get it out. I needed to share this sin and struggle I had endured last night. I needed the words to be in the air so that someone else could be there with me. The fear of keeping it all to myself was too great. If no one knew, then it could happen again. If no one knew, it *would* happen again.

So I replayed the events of the previous night to Annie, just as I've shared them with you, except with tears streaming down my face. Was it embarrassing? Of course it was. Not many people talk about it, which makes it even harder to say out loud. I felt like a fraud, a fake, as if God could never use me again—certainly not as a teacher to other women that morning! (I know, drastic, but it's how I was feeling.)

But my sweet friend Annie never faltered when I was telling her this. Her eyes never looked at me with sin-shocked disgust. She never portrayed that she was repulsed by me and my actions from the night before. She only looked at me with the eyes of a friend who knows that Jesus is bigger than my struggle.

She spoke truth over me that morning, easing the shame I was feeling. She reminded me that I was a daughter of the King, and that nothing I'd done could take that away. She repeated to me the exact truths I would soon be teaching the women at our church that morning—that my identity was not based on anything I had done or hadn't done, but on everything that Jesus had done for me. She reminded me of a verse I've already shared with you, but it's one of my favorites so I don't mind repeating it: "There is therefore now no condemnation for those who are in Christ Jesus" (Rom. 8:1)—meaning, the struggle that you're walking through, the sin that keeps creeping up, Jesus died for that. It's not a surprise to Him. It didn't get left off the list of sins that He bore on the cross. It was there. That sin was taken care of. We still fight like crazy not to submit to it again, but we have complete confidence that when we fall, when our flesh wins, we are forgiven—"no condemnation." We are still valuable to the work of God. Our sins don't define us; only the blood of Jesus does.

Annie told me all of those things that morning, before we prayed together and celebrated what Christ had done for *all* of us.

Then I stood before the women of my church that day and taught them with a confidence that was stronger because of the love that my friend Annie showed me when I opened up to her about my sin and my struggle. She listened to me, she validated my confession, she encouraged me to repent, and then I walked out of that room confident in the forgiveness that God offers me. She was never once shocked by my sin. Disheartened and broken, for sure. But not shocked.

Thank God I'd been willing to be vulnerable.

Something beautiful happens when we're vulnerable.

In disclosing my struggle to my friend that day, I was so extremely vulnerable before her. It wasn't the first time I had shared hard things with her, or that she had shared hard things with me. We have a history together of being able to do that, so I was fairly confident how she would react. I knew she would be a safe place for me to land.

But becoming vulnerable with friends in many cases can be downright scary and intimidating, to say the least. What if you open up and it goes bad? What if you invite someone into your pain and they don't carry it with the tenderness and dignity that you think it deserves? The risk and fear of exposure is always there.

Plus, it's exhausting. How much is too much? What do they really want to know? When your neighbor asks, "How was your morning?" do they really want to know that you spilled an entire carafe of coffee on your new rug? Or that your dog ate a hundred-dollar bill? Or that one of your kids peed in the bed the night before? Or that you wish you were on a Caribbean island with no kids at all? (All of those things may or may not have happened to me before!) Do they want to hear that? Nope, they don't. So we say, "I'm fine, thank you."

When you meet with your girlfriends, and they share about a woman at the office who just left her husband for another man, do you dare open up and tell them your daydreams involving yourself and the waiter from your favorite coffee shop? When someone says they missed you at church or some other event, do you tell them the truth—that you were having one of your anxiety attacks and couldn't seem to make yourself leave the house?

You see, we are scared of opening up. What will they think? What will they do with this information they've learned about us? So we convince ourselves they wouldn't understand. We convince ourselves they'd be weirded out by our struggles. Or we convince ourselves that nobody really cares enough to want to hear about it anyway, even if we were willing to say it.

But being vulnerable is not (as we sometimes think) the same as being helpless, defenseless, and weak. Vulnerability within a relationship is what keeps you close. Being vulnerable with someone says to them that you value them, that you welcome them into your life. All the parts. The good, the bad, and the ugly.

Yet of all the positive, redemptive things I could say about the value of being open and honest with others, here's the biggest one I've learned over the years . . .

Vulnerability leads to vulnerability.

When you're vulnerable with your friends, you give them permission to be vulnerable with *you*. When you make the awkward first move and share your true feelings, you set the tone for the relationship.

Of course there will be times when this goes bad and feels weird, but finding friends that you can be vulnerable with is worth every ounce of fear you might endure. It's also worth every amount of trial and error. If you open up to a friend and it goes worse than you expected, then maybe this isn't the kind of friend you need to be in a close relationship with. Maybe they aren't quite ready to carry this weight, or maybe they've just never experienced vulnerability between friends before and, therefore, they don't know how to handle it.

But being vulnerable with someone has a way of breaking down walls. It has a way of bringing people together. Do you ever wonder how you can spend one week with someone on a life-altering trip and become better friends with them than with someone you've known for ten years? It's because you allowed them into your world. You shared your fears, hopes, dreams, and maybe so much more together. You were *vulnerable* with them. And now they're friends for life.

I have girlfriends to whom I can tell anything—and I do mean anything—and they will listen, direct me to truth, and fight with me to the end. Amy and I have been friends for over twenty-five years and have walked through lots of life together. Maris, Laura, Kim, Annie, and I have all been brought together through our husbands' making music together. Amanda, Tiffany, and I met in an intensive discipleship class at church and became fast friends. Noelle and I met and bonded over adoption. She's heard me at some of my weakest parenting moments, and I've been let into some of her lowest moments as well.

These ladies get me. They know me. I can send them a message that says I'm struggling with something, and they won't text/ call/email me back with a cute little saying about picking myself up by my big-girl panties or something like that. Nope, not at all. These girls speak truth to me. They tell me who I am and Whose I am. They remind me of the hope we share in the gospel. They remind me I'm in relationship with a Savior who has never left me and never will.

I can be vulnerable with these friends because I trust they love me. I know they have my best in mind, and I know they are tethered well to the truth of God's Word. They aren't going to feed me any nonsense about being a better person or whatnot. They're going to love me and feed me truths from the Scripture. That's it. Our *individual* vulnerability has led to our *collective* vulnerability—and to friendships that are healthy, supportive, challenging (in a good way), and real.

Now, this didn't happen overnight for us. You can't expect friendships like these to do that, where women are vulnerable and open with each other. These kinds of friendships are developed through seasons: seasons of togetherness, seasons of sorrow, seasons of rejoicing, seasons of pain. Instead of going through those seasons by ourselves—alone and guarded—we've gone through them with our stories out in the open, with our struggles a common topic of conversation.

I think many women have been hurt in friendships before, and that's what keeps us from opening up. Maybe you *did* open up that one time to a friend, somebody you thought you could trust. But lo and behold, she wasn't trustworthy and your heart was damaged. Your vulnerability was used against you in the end. I'm not saying it can't happen.

I'm wondering, though, if you could try again . . . if you could give your friendships another chance . . . because when you're real with people, you provide them a great opportunity to love you and point you to the truth. But when you're fake with people, hiding your junk and putting on a perceived look of perfection, you rob those around you of the honor of showing you love and pointing you to Jesus.

Wouldn't you love being that kind of friend for other people? Maybe your own fear of vulnerability is what's keeping you from it.

If there are two words I've heard more than any others when people describe me or talk about my podcast, *The Happy Hour with Jamie Ivey*, it's that I'm (1) authentic and (2) vulnerable. What I suspect people feel when they're listening to the show is that they are getting the real me, and that I'm willing to expose myself to them in an accurate way.

I sure hope this is true of me. But I need you to know, this did not happen all at once. Since you are this far along in the book, you've seen all the insecurities, self-doubt, uncertainty, and lack of self-confidence I've walked through. I lived so many years trying to be something I wasn't. Trying to earn people's approval. Trying to look like a "good Christian girl" during times when I don't know if I even was a Christian, and even in times when I was.

In fact, being a new believer was the time in my life when I was the most scared to death of what people would think of me, if they only knew the *real me.* I was never vulnerable and authentic with anyone. The perceived cost was too great to me. What they might possibly think about me was too much for my weary soul to bear. My identity—in my mind, at least—was still too tied up in what other people were saying or thinking about me. And whenever that happens, when that's the way you see yourself, you protect yourself at all costs.

The problem was, I couldn't keep it up. The persona of having everything together became too heavy to carry. But what I found was—when I was able to be the real me, with all my failures and successes—I became more free in Christ. I was able to point people to Jesus and show them all the ways He had forgiven me. I found in being vulnerable that I was bringing glory to God by showing all the ways that I needed Him.

And what's even cooler than that (if I can even imagine such a thing) is that by being willing to open up with others about the parts of my life that are hard, God used my vulnerability to make space for others to open up as well. Then the goodness of God just started to multiply all around me, with God getting more and more glory through more and more people.

And this same incredible experience is available to you . . . to everybody.

Recently, I was interviewing a woman on my podcast who is currently in those hard parenting ages with her kids, two of which have special needs—making it doubly hard, triply hard. I thanked her for opening up and sharing with my listeners and me about her struggles, her pain, her successes, her failures, because I assured her she was allowing room for someone else to open up about their own struggles as well. When we bring ourselves fully to the table, it says to others that they are welcome as well. God uses the stories of His people to change the world. It's true. Your story can change the world, but you first must be willing to share it.

Now, when I talk about being vulnerable, I'm not saying it's always some huge revelation you need to unload on somebody, dredging up another wretched skeleton from your closet. There are times and places for that, sure, and that's definitely a big part of what I mean. We can't keep that stuff locked away or else it will tear us up from the inside, spawning all kinds of other sins and struggles and, worse, restricting our freedom to glorify God through what His grace has done within us. But in order to experience maximum freedom, vulnerability simply needs to become our lifestyle—being vulnerable about the day-to-day. When my friends hear that I'm having a hard time loving my husband or kids today (yes, we all know this actually happens in life!), they see I'm a real person, just like them, and pretty soon we're all coming clean on our everyday struggles and areas of weakness and times when we don't always make the best decisions.

It's why we as moms are drawn to blogs entitled, "I'm Not Making My Kids' Lunches This Year," or "Five Ways to Screw Up Christmas for Your Kids," or "The Day I Forgot to Feed My Kids Dinner." All of those articles scream to the reader, "I'M A NORMAL MOM AND MESS UP ALL THE TIME TOO," and we love that. We love seeing the realness in someone's life.

You might be one who's scared to show people your realness. You're perceived as someone who always has it together, who's never missed a school party, who's never late to work, and who always makes her bed. What happens, though, when you feel as though you *aren't* meeting these crazy expectations you've set for yourself? What happens when you fear that someone might find out you *don't*, in fact, have it all together? You are scared of anyone knowing the truth because you feel comfortable in this perceived perfection life you're living.

Well, here's my tip of the week for you. If I was putting the best spin on this whole "perceived perfection" thing, I'd say it's what you do to avoid letting other people down. Because you never let people down. Because you're "perfect." (Which we all know is impossible because no one's ever been perfect besides Jesus, even though many women are trying their hardest to be Jesus 2.0, and it's not working.) But I guarantee, you will let people down less often when they expect you to make mistakes than when you're maintaining the illusion of being practically flawless. You'll have a much easier time giving people grace, and you'll learn that nothing in life is better than receiving grace.

When I finally began to be vulnerable with my friends about my past, the difference was both life-changing and life-giving. As they confirmed the work God had done and was doing in my life, I began to feel more freedom to be me. "If they only knew" became "they know it all." And you know what? That's the best place to live in the whole world.

By opening up with Annie about the struggle I'd had with porn that night, it made Satan need to work a whole lot harder trying to find an opening to exploit in my heart like that again. And when Annie has opened up to me about struggles in her own life, she's been able to see new patterns of victory develop as well. But the next struggle is always right around the corner, and we'll need each other's help in fighting that one too. By staying authentic, by being vulnerable, by being free from putting on an act, we can pick ourselves up from our mistakes, talk about them, and move on with new confidence and strength—because of Jesus.

We need to fight for each other. Believe in each other. Listen to each other. Pray for each other. When we become women who own our stories and become vulnerable about our lives, Jesus' grace and mercy take center stage. And when Jesus is at the center instead of our perfectly polished selves, we can stand before Him, our husbands, our children, and our girlfriends, let out all of our junk, and know He will get the glory, not us.

Being vulnerable—sharing our need for a Savior—points people to Jesus and not ourselves. And He's who they need to be looking at, not us!

Chapter 10

Jesus Is Better

I t's hard to watch people you love limping through life because of past mistakes. They never get over what they did so many years ago and, therefore, their entire life is wrecked. Everything hinged on that one choice. I've seen it play out time and time again in friends' lives, in the women I meet at events, in people everywhere. The feelings of guilt and shame never seem to go away.

I even suspect that sometimes these people don't know how to function outside of feeling guilt and shame. They believe they've taken up their cross in life, which means being forever ashamed and guilty over what they've done. Staying in those emotions is the only way they feel worthy of being loved by God. His love and acceptance, they think, is contingent on their continued investment of shame and guilt. They seem to think that if they walked in freedom—the freedom that God truly offers—they would be saying, in effect, that they didn't really believe what they did was wrong.

This thinking is so jacked up and anti-gospel, yet many of us get stuck here and don't know how to get out. This whole book has been the story of my journey through this gauntlet. Have I arrived? Goodness gracious, no. I'm still such a messed-up person. My arrival will not happen until after I take my last breath here on this earth and open up my eyes to see my precious Jesus waiting for me. That's arrival. And not a moment sooner.

Yet I can say confidently that I no longer dwell in shame and guilt. Do I feel it? For sure. I *should* feel it. It's part of the warning system that God has built into our hearts, letting us know when we're on the wrong track, when we're sinning against Him. But I don't stay there. In guilt and shame. I *can't* anymore. I've experienced the freedom that comes from confession, repentance, and vulnerability, and I refuse to go back to living a life of "perceived perfection." It's not worth it to me. I'd rather you know all of my junk than try my hardest every day to keep up a persona so that you don't know the real me. That's exhausting, and I won't do it anymore.

But I'm thinking right now of a dear friend who lives in shame and guilt. Years ago, he made a decision that altered his family's life forever. He chose to have an affair, and with that one decision, the consequences poured in. He lost trust from his children, his wife suffered, and guilt flooded his soul with intense waves. Praise be to God and God alone, his marriage survived, his kids forgave him, and life moved on. God was gracious to forgive him, and he lived to fight another day . . . except that he's too often been fighting a losing battle. He's squandered a lot of time during this life, fighting a battle that's already been fought.

I've heard him declare many times over the years, "I know in my heart that God forgives me, but I just can't forgive myself." I'm certain you've heard this statement before. You might even have uttered it yourself at one point or another—when you've felt as though your sin or failure or weakness was so big, you could never forgive yourself.

I've heard my ladies at the jail make this statement often, especially when they talk about how their crimes are affecting their children. It's one thing when we make decisions that hurt ourselves, but what about when those decisions directly hurt the people we were supposed to protect and provide for, who don't have any substitute for the role we were meant to play in their lives? These women's kids are being forced to survive without their momma in their lives on a regular basis. And when you're separated from your children for years like that, for no other reason than your own foolish choices, forgiving yourself is hard to muster up.

My friend struggles with this too—not being able to forgive himself for his decision and for the immense hurt it caused those around him.

What if I proposed to you, however, that we were never meant to forgive ourselves? I know it sounds a bit off, but think about it for a minute. It's not our job to forgive ourselves. We can't. We don't have the power. We don't have the ability. We don't have the right standing with God for that. *Forgive ourselves*? Really? How would anybody actually go about doing that?

If you could forgive yourself, there would be no need for Jesus, right? And if there's no need for Jesus, then this whole Christianity thing is false and we have wasted our lives.

In my brain, I really do get where these feelings are coming from. You might feel as though you somehow owe God a life of shame because of the choices you've made. Yet at the same time, the Bible is full of Scripture saying the exact opposite. God's Word tells us that God sent His Son for us, to forgive us, to offer us new life, to redeem us, to bring us back to Him. How is anything we could ever do supposed to improve upon that?

If you're feeling as though you just can't forgive yourself today, I want to say to you in the firmest, yet kindest pastor's wife voice I can possibly make: "YOU CAN'T, SO STOP TRYING." When you walk around feeling as though you still need to forgive yourself, what you're saying to God is that His sacrifice wasn't enough.

His only Son dying on a cross for your sins wasn't enough. More is needed for you to feel forgiven. So, by your continual yearning to forgive yourself, you are actually creating a life where Jesus' blood and sacrifice aren't enough, leaving yourself essentially a works-based religion to follow, where if you could just do a few more "good things," you could possibly begin to forgive yourself.

See any problem with that? Of course you do. You know what I'm saying is true. But I'll bet, within the few moments it's taken for you to read this one tiny paragraph, you've already begun coming up with excuses for why your situation is different and why the same gospel parameters don't apply.

This is where we as Christians begin to live in bondage. We become shackled to our sins, our pasts, and our regrets, instead of shackled to Jesus, whose "yoke is easy" and whose "burden is light" (Matt. 11:30). We become ruled and dominated by what we've done, rather than freed for abundant life by what Jesus has done.

My friend who is waddling around in his shame, regret, guilt, and "unforgiveness" has missed out on years of abundant joy. He's continually looking to God and proclaiming (in words he would never actually say out loud), "Thanks for these promises and all, but I pass. I'd rather sit here in my guilt and shame. Isn't that what I deserve? Isn't that what You want of me?"

No. It isn't.

A life of guilt and shame does not proclaim the goodness of God; it proclaims the impotence and inadequacy of God. *He can do a lot,* we say from inside our sadness and self-pity, *but I've proven to be too tough a challenge for Him.* What prideful people we are to think that we are actually *too much* for God.

I'm sorry, but I don't think your best attempts at being good enough to feel forgiven are going to be better than what Jesus has done. In this way and a million others, (say it with me . . .)

Jesus is better.

My friend isn't living as though Jesus is better. Nothing in all his guilt and shame is giving off the impression that Jesus is better. All I'm hearing is that God came up a little short on this one. So why would anyone look at my friend's life—based on how well he's learning to apply the grace of God to his heart—and say, "I believe there's hope for me in this Jesus that I hear about."

The reason why I want to be an open book is not so I can say, "Look at me," but because I want to say—in every way possible— "Look at Him!" Look at all the ways He has used me in spite of my stupidity. Look at all the ways He has endured with me, even through my many self-inflicted sorrows in life. Look at all the ways He has blessed me, even when others would have given up on me. I want to constantly shout, "JESUS IS BETTER!"

Way better than anything else *I've* got.

I love how the book of Hebrews speaks to this. The author of this book from the New Testament spends so much time telling us how much better Jesus is than anything or anyone else. He's better than the Law; He's better than the priesthood; His new covenant with us is better than the old one. He is our only hope not to remain unclean forever.

Hebrews 9, for example, talks about how we are cleansed through the blood of Jesus, not like in the past through the blood sacrifice of animals. In the Old Testament, before Jesus came, the high priest would go in once a year with the blood of animals and offer it as a sacrifice to God to purify the people from their sins. But every year a new sacrifice had to be made. The people weren't clean for a lifetime, only for a year.

When you think about how you believe God handles your sin, are you still sort of living out the practices of the Old Testament? Continually trying to make amends for the sins in your life? Every year (every month, every week, every day), you're always trying harder, working to atone for your mistakes. I can picture my friend feeling this way, fighting to do better, year after year, hoping he might somehow feel forgiven eventually.

But get this . . .

> But when Christ appeared as a high priest of the good
> things that have come, then through the greater and
> more perfect tent (not made with hands, that is, not
> of this creation) he entered once for all into the holy
> places, not by means of the blood of goats and calves
> but by means of his own blood, thus securing an eternal
> redemption. (Heb. 9:11–12)

Did you spot some of the "better" words in there? Jesus is the
high priest of "good things," appearing in a "greater" tabernacle, a
"more perfect" place, doing a better job of making atonement than
animal blood could ever do.

> For if the blood of goats and bulls, and the sprinkling
> of defiled persons with the ashes of a heifer, sanctify for
> the purification of the flesh, how much more will the
> blood of Christ, who through the eternal Spirit offered
> himself without blemish to God, purify our conscience
> from dead works to serve the living God. (Heb. 9:13–14)

Yeah, "how much more" can His blood "purify our conscience
from dead works"—which, by the way, are the only kind of works
we're able to offer—so that we can "serve the living God"? And
isn't serving Him the only right response of someone who's been

so completely forgiven of their sins? Do shame and guilt do that? Do they help us serve Him well and faithfully?

Saying, "I'm not good enough," and leaving it there doesn't present a whole gospel. Yet saying, "I'm not good enough, but Jesus is better," proclaims the hope that lifts you out of the bondage of feeling unforgiven and transforms your life into a megaphone of the whole gospel message to others.

Listen, if I've come off sounding too blunt here, I hope you haven't taken it that way. I can sympathize all too well with being overwhelmed by guilt and watching it burrow down into shame. I just hope you've seen through this book—as perhaps you've seen time and again in your own life—that guilt and shame make for a hard place to set up house in. They come with constant worry, constant anxiety, constant depression, and a constant need to do more. Shame never brings freedom. But Christ came to purify our conscience. God always knew the sacrifices in the Old Testament were not enough. We needed more. We needed a perfect sacrifice to actually take on our sin, in order that we could be fully clean. All those sacrifices in the Old Testament were leading up to the one true and final sacrifice in Jesus. He is the only One who can take that stain away. Jesus deals finally and fully with our guilty conscience, which is what's under attack when we feel shame.

See why there's no need to keep living in it? See why you can feel released from all the hard work of forgiving yourself?

See why Jesus, as always, is better?

Shame over past sins that have already been forgiven is not from God. No matter how much you go to church, or read your Bible, or give away lots of money, you're not improving on Christ's forgiveness of you. Certainly, those are good things that will come as an overflow of your faith. They're evidence that you're giving Him a stronger hold on your surrendered heart. But you can just sit back now and rejoice in the fact that "while we were still sinners, Christ died for us" (Rom. 5:8). His death brought you into a relationship with God and secured your eternity with Him. This isn't just *good* news, isn't just *church-sounding* news; this is *freeing* news—believing that what God says is actually true. You can live your life now as a forgiven person, based on what He's already done and said, and not on what you may feel about yourself.

A few years ago, my husband and his friend Brett wrote a song that our church has grown to love, as well as churches around the world. I know why it resonates with me, and I think it's the same for everyone else who belts it out as well. The song is called "Jesus Is Better," and each time I sing it, I'm reminded that what the Bible says about Him is true, even when I'm not sure I know how to believe it and hold on to it.

This reminds me of a story in the New Testament where a father approached Jesus, asking Him to cast a demon out of his son. "If you can do anything," this father begged, "have compassion on us and help us." To which Jesus answered, repeating the man's words, "'If you can'? Everything is possible for the one who believes." The father's response, however, is what I find myself saying and wanting so often as well. "Immediately the father of the boy cried out, 'I do believe; help my unbelief!'" (Mark 9:22–24). That's what I feel when I sing this song. *Lord, help me believe!*

Throughout many seasons in my life, I've needed to recite things to myself so my heart would continue to believe them. When a family finds out that sexual abuse has occurred within their home, I have to remind myself that God wasn't surprised by this and has not forsaken anyone who's been harmed by such betrayal. When our friend's daughter, who they've been fostering for many months, is sent back to a home that we believe is not safe, I must remind my heart that God loves this little girl more than any of us ever can. When someone who has led me in ministry confesses to a sin with lasting consequences, I'm reminded that God is my only leader, and that He will never fail me. Sometimes we must proclaim things with our lips as a way of reinforcing them in our hearts.

And "Jesus Is Better" is that kind of song for me. Part of it goes like this . . .

In all my sorrows, Jesus is better—make my heart believe.

In every vict'ry, Jesus is better—make my heart believe.

Than any comfort, Jesus is better—make my heart believe.

More than all riches, Jesus is better—make my heart believe.

Our souls declaring, Jesus is better—make my heart believe.

Our song eternal, Jesus is better—make my heart believe.[7]

Singing this song over and over for the past several years has helped me worship God through the remembrance that no matter what, He is better. I don't need to live in shame and guilt—Jesus is better. No matter what I've done in life, I can walk in forgiveness—Jesus is better. I'm not held in bondage to my past—Jesus is better.

Jesus is better.

Be reminded of that today.

Jesus frequently reminded His disciples about the things that matter most in life. Many times, He had to reset their affections on kingdom things instead of on earthly things. Right before He pursued the cross, He gathered His boys around Himself and gave them an incredible illustration to remember . . .

He said to them, "I have earnestly desired to eat this Passover with you before I suffer. For I tell you, I will not eat it until it is fulfilled in the kingdom of God." And he took a cup, and when he had given thanks he said, "Take this, and divide it among yourselves. For I tell you that from now on I will not drink of the fruit of the vine until the kingdom of God comes."

And he took bread, and when he had given thanks, he broke it and gave it to them, saying, "This is my body, which is given for you. Do this in remembrance of me."

And likewise the cup after they had eaten, saying, "This cup that is poured out for you is the new covenant in my blood." (Luke 22:15–20)

"Do this in remembrance of me." Remember. Remember.

Faithfulness to Him comes from remembering all He's done for you. His entire Word is a reminder of all He's done for you. My whole reason for writing out this story of how God redeemed someone who looked so unredeemable, and how He continues pursuing me until I look more like Him, is to help you *remember*, through what He's done for me, what He's done and can do for you.

For in remembering, you find the fullness of your forgiveness.

In remembering, you find your freedom.

In remembering, you can live radically for Him.

About a year ago, I was attending a service that my husband was leading for all of his staff on the worship team. Using these same verses from Luke 22, he talked about our need to keep remembering throughout our lifetime what Jesus has done for us. But he also used this passage to show that our God is communal. Jesus' desire around the table that night was not only that His followers would receive His word as individuals but as a community.

Aaron was specifically speaking to the community in front of him, of course, but I want to talk to you. I'm a part of your community now because of spending these few hours together as you've been reading this book. (And goodness gracious, I shared some vulnerable pieces of my life and invited you in!) God has set up community to be a place where we remind each other of His faithfulness to us. Where we remind each other of all that God has done in our lives, and as we tell each other, our hearts start to believe more and more that what His Word says is true. We have the history of God to bank on. He can be nothing but faithful to His children—it's a part of His character. He can be nothing but kind to His children—it's a part of His character. He can be nothing but full of grace to those who follow Him—it's a part of His character.

I want you to look around and think about your own community. Who do you do life with? Who are your people? Community matters in reminding us of the truths that Jesus is better. And as you think about your community—whether one you've already established or one you *need* to establish—I challenge you to see your role among these people in a new way.

Instead of trying to be better than the rest of them, become willing to confess your sins and struggles with them.

Instead of being appalled at their failures and inadequacies, become a safe person for them to share their worst fears and shortcomings with.

Instead of using them as a more accurate indicator of your identity than the one that Christ has already given you, become anchored in the unchanging truth of His Word.

But instead of thinking you can make it just fine without them, become convinced that your ability to put His Word into practice and bring maximum glory to God is through humbly serving Him together and serving each other, not in staying aloof and keeping up pretenses.

Early monastic followers of God received Communion in a unique way. When they gathered around the table, they were given a glass of wine and a chunk of bread, and were each asked to say two things. First, they were to testify to the faithfulness of God in their life. Second, they were to confess their sin and their need for Him. Then at the end of each person's statement of confession, everyone in unison spoke aloud the words, "ME TOO," reminding each other that they were experiencing Communion with God together as sinful people, saved by grace. As they took a bite of bread and remembered His body crushed for them . . . as they drank the wine and remembered the blood of Jesus poured out for them . . . they remembered also that as members of this community, none was better than another. All were equally in need before the fountain of God's mercy. Only *Jesus* was better.

I want us to be a generation of women willing to say, "Me too"—that I get your pain, I get your struggle, I get your sorrow, I get your weariness. Know why? Because it's mine too. "Me too." When you see a friend who's battling, when someone confesses sin to you, sit with them, listen to them, point them to Jesus, and quietly say to them, "Me too."

The pages of this book are drenched with "me too" tears, poured out over a so-far lifetime of failing and following, failing and following. Yet God has forgiven me, just as God has forgiven you. And even on days where we may see more losing than winning, His faithfulness and forgiveness will hold us together.

For as bad as it's been, and as bad as it can get, Jesus is better.

Let us all be women who believe that to be true.

Notes

1. John Piper, "The Good End of Godly Regret," www.desiringgod.org/messages/the-good-end-of-godly-regret.
2. "Come, Thou Fount," public domain.
3. Ibid.
4. Ibid.
5. Ibid.
6. Edward T. Welch, *Shame Interrupted* (Greensboro, NC: New Growth Press, 2012), 35.
7. "Jesus Is Better" written by Aaron Ivey and Brett Land © 2013 by Austin Stone Music (ASCAP).

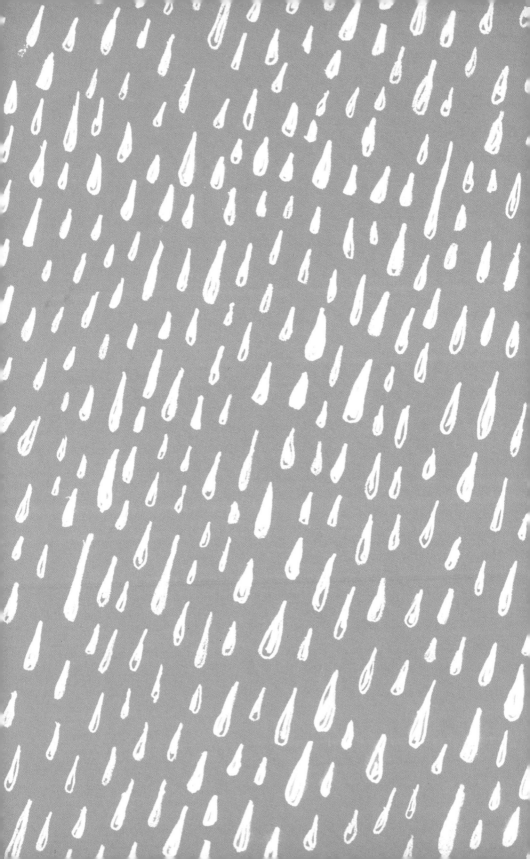